Financial Management and
Analysis
Workbook

T0340143

THE FRANK J. FABOZZI SERIES

This workbook is the companion, self-study guide to *Financial Management and Analysis: Second Edition*.

Please visit www.WileyFinance.com for more information.

Financial Management and Analysis

Analysis

Workbook

Step-by-Step Exercises and Tests to Help You Master
Financial Management and Analysis

PAMELA P. PETERSON

FRANK J. FABOZZI

WENDY D. HABEGGER

WILEY

John Wiley & Sons, Inc.

For general information on our other products and services, or technical support, please contact our Customer Care Department within the United States at 800-762-2974, outside the United States at 317-572-3993, or fax 317-572-4002.

Wiley also publishes its books in a variety of electronic formats. Some content that appears in print may not be available in electronic books.

For more information about Wiley, visit our web site at www.wiley.com.

ISBN: 0-471-47761-3

10 9 8 7 6 5 4 3 2 1

Contents

PART TWO

Solutions   289

Questions and Problems

CHAPTER 1

Introduction to Financial Management and Analysis

FILL IN THE BLANKS

Refer to Chapter 1, pages 3–24 in *Financial Management and Analysis*.

1. _____ is the application of economic principles and concepts to business decisions and problem solving. It can be divided into three categories: _____, _____, and _____. _____ is the management of a firm's cash flow to increase shareholder wealth.

2. _____ and _____ are decisions made concerning financial management. Financial managers compare potential _____ and _____, otherwise known as expected returns. The uncertainty inherent with these returns is referred to as the _____.

3. The evaluation of the financial condition and operating performance of a business firm, industry, and economy, and future forecasting of its condition and performance is known as _____. It is also used to evaluate specific _____ and _____ within a firm and the overall _____ and _____ outside the firm.

4. _____, _____, and _____ are the three major forms of business organizations. The _____ provides the largest percentage of U.S. business incomes, but the majority of businesses are _____. Proprietors and _____ partners are liable for only business debts, whereas _____ partners and the owners of a(n) _____ stand to lose only the initial investment.

5. The _____ are the contract between the shareholders and corporation and authorizes the corporation to issue stock. The _____ of a corporation are rules of governance. The owners of a corporation are also called the _____. They elect a(n) _____ for representative purposes in the major business decisions. A(n) _____ corporation is owned by a multitude of share holders while a(n) _____ is owned by a few shareholders. Corporations whose shares are publicly traded must file financial statements with the _____.

6. _____ and _____ business income are subject to the personal income tax rate of the individual owners, whereas a(n) _____ pays taxes as a separate legal entity. Cash distributions to shareholders are also taxed as personal income of the owner, leading to what is known as _____.

7. A hybrid form of business is a(n) _____ and it combines the best features of a(n) _____ and a(n) _____. These types of businesses are treated as a partnership for _____ purposes, while the owners are not _____ for firm obligations. A(n) _____ is a popular form of business that is commenced by a group of persons or entities for a specific business activity in which the relationship only lasts the length of the activity. It may also be structured as a(n) _____ or a(n) _____ and is treated according to how it is structured.

8. The single financial goal is to maximize the _____ wealth, which means to maximize the _____ of a share of stock for a corporation. The market value of shareholders' equity is the product of the price of _____ and the number of _____, which are the total number of shares owned by shareholders. The stock price is equal to the _____ of all expected future cash flows to owners. In a(n) _____, the price of a stock reflects all publicly available information so the investor is unlikely to earn _____ profits by trading on information already known to the public. The only

way for an investor to increase the return is to increase the
_____.

9. _____ profit is the difference between revenues
and costs, where costs are the unambiguous costs of doing
business. _____ profits include both explicit and
implicit costs. Maximization of _____ profits
maximizes owners' wealth.

10. A(n) _____ is a person acting in the best interest
of another person or group of people. The _____
is the person or group being represented. Three types of
agency costs are _____, _____, and
_____. Interests of management and sharehold-
ers are aligned when executive compensation packages
are designed to encourage _____-term investment by managers in the stock of the corporation. In particular, _____ and _____ might be
the better forms of compensation as they require the manager to be an owner in the corporation and hold stock for
a specified time.

SHORT ANSWER QUESTIONS

Refer to Chapter 1, pages 3–24 in *Financial Management and Analysis*.

1. According to market efficiency, if investors who trade on publicly available information are unlikely to earn abnormal profits, then should small investors not invest in the stock market?

2. What are accounting profits or economic profits and which one should an investor be more concerned with?

3. Why might a restricted option compensation program be more effective than a performance shares program in motivating managers to maximize the wealth of the owners?

4. An article in today's *Wall Street Journal* states a certain drug company has received approval from the Federal Food and Drug Administration to market a new medication for people with heart disease. You believe you should call your broker and invest in the stock of this company immediately because it will undoubtedly increase in value. Given what you know about efficient markets, what advice do you suspect you will receive from your broker?

5. Annie and Alice invested $50,000 and $25,000 respectively in a business enterprise. During the first year of operation, the business had taxable income of $12,000.

   a. If the business is organized as a partnership, with profits and losses shared based on the proportion of each partner's original investment, how much of the income will each claim on her personal tax return?

   b. After the initial year of success, a weakened economy caused the business to falter. Following four successive years of losses, the assets of the business were $30,000 and the debts were $50,000. The two owners decided to liquidate the business. What are the financial consequences of the dissolution of the business to each owner?

c. If the business had been a limited partnership, with Annie being the general partner who actively ran the business, what would the financial consequences be for each owner?

d. If the business had been a corporation with ownership interests based on the proportion of each woman's initial investment, what would the financial consequences be for each owner?

CHAPTER 2

Securities and Markets

FILL IN THE BLANKS

Refer to Chapter 2, pages 27–47 in *Financial Management and Analysis*.

1. A(n) _____ is a claim on future cash flows. A(n) _____ is a where securities are bought and sold. Securities are classified into three groups: _____ securities, _____ securities, and _____ securities. _____ securities have a one year or less original maturity. _____ securities are long-term securities issued by corporations and governments.

2. _____ is short-term debt of a large corporation with good credit standing. A(n) _____ is the U.S. government's short-term debt. _____ certificates of deposit are issued by large _____ and are often transferred among investors.

3. _____ is the ownership interest in a corporation. _____ are the called the residual owners of the firm. Common stock has _____ maturity. Cash payments to shareholders are called _____. _____ stockholders are guaranteed a fixed dividend, but are not residual owners of the firm.

4. On a debt security, the _____ refers to the borrowed monetary amount. The _____ are periodic payments. Debt securities with less than 10 years to maturity are called _____. _____ bonds are debt of state and local governments. These bonds interest payments are exempted from _____ taxes. _____ bonds are backed by the issuer's taxing power. _____ bonds are backed by the proceeds of a specific project. Bond trading is mostly done in the _____ market, although small orders are traded on _____.

5. The _____ market is where new capital is raised, whereas the _____ market is where a shift in funds occurs between investors. Capital is raised in the primary market through _____, which are direct sales of the issues to investors, and through _____ agreements, which are when investment bankers purchase the securities for immediate resale to the public.

6. _____ are actual physical markets in which shares are traded. Transactions in the _____ market occur over computers and phone lines. The organized exchanges in the U.S. are _____ owned. Exchanges in other countries are often controlled by _____ or _____. There is U.S. government regulation of the financial markets. In particular, The Securities Act of 1933 requires that new securities be

_____. The Securities and Exchange Act of 1934 established the _____ Commission.

7. The largest exchange in the United States in terms of market value of the shares traded is the _____. The other national exchange is the _____. There are seven _____ exchanges that trade _____ listed securities. The largest over-the-counter market for common stock is known as _____ and it is a computerized quotation system. The larger, most actively traded securities in NASDAQ are included in the _____. The NASDAQ system is the _____ largest market for securities. The Dow Jones Industrial Average is computed using _____ stocks. The S&P 500 is an index of _____ companies' stocks.

8. A(n) _____ market is one where asset prices quickly reflect all information that is available. _____ form market efficiency means current prices reflect all past prices so investors cannot earn _____ profits based on past price movements. The _____ form of market efficiency indicates security prices incorporate all information that is available to the public. Empirical evidence suggests that U.S. security markets are _____ form efficient. _____ form market efficiency implies investors will not earn abnormal profits trading on information that is private. Recent events suggest abnormal profits may be gained by _____ trading.

SHORT ANSWER QUESTIONS

Refer to Chapter 2, pages 27–47 in *Financial Management and Analysis.*

1. How do stocks differ from bonds?

2. How do common stocks differ from preferred stock?

3. What are the similar and differing characteristics between general obligation bonds and revenue bonds?

4. What type of investor would prefer stocks to bonds and why? (Consider the answers for questions 1, 2, and 3.)

5. How do exchanges and over-the-counter markets differ?

CHAPTER 3

Financial Institutions and the Cost of Money

FILL IN THE BLANKS

Refer to Chapter 3, pages 49–80 in *Financial Management and Analysis*.

1. In the United States, there is a central monetary authority known as the _____ and it acts as the U.S. _____ bank. The main function of a central bank is to implement _____ policy which controls the availability of _____ funds.

2. The interaction between the _____ and _____ for currency influences the _____ rates paid to _____ funds and the amount of _____ earned on _____ funds. The _____ for money is dictated by the availability of _____ opportunities. The _____ of money is determined by a nation's central bank's actions.

3. _____ cash, sometimes called _____, _____, or _____, is money created _____ and functions beyond the scope of banks, checks, coin, and currency overseen by the _____. Electronic cash is rapidly gaining in popularity over more traditional _____, _____, and _____. It is more convenient than other forms of money and results in a reduction of _____ costs for businesses.

4. _____ provide services such as financial intermediaries that alter _____ assets purchased in the market and reformulate them into more desirable _____. Financial institutions provide _____, _____, and _____ advice and manage _____ for all types of investors.

5. Corporate financing involves _____ funds for a bank's customers and providing _____ on such matters as _____ for obtaining funds, corporate _____, divestitures, and _____.

6. Banks are _____ and _____ by several _____ and _____ governments. An encompassing _____ in bank regulation in recent years has been the _____ Act of 1999, also known as the _____ Act. It allows a financial holding company to engage in _____ and _____ securities.

7. The _____ market makes available the _____ issued _____ by corporations and other entities seeking to _____ funds. The firm issuing a security is the _____. The investors working with issuers to _____ these securities are called _____.

8. _____ activities are regulated by the _____ Commission. The Securities Act of 1933 governs _____ and requires that a(n) _____ statement and _____ statements be filed with the SEC.

9. Money is not a free _____. Those who _____ money are willing to _____ for it and those who _____ money expect to be _____. The _____ is the cost of money; the _____ the demand for money. The _____ the interest rate; the _____ the demand, the _____ the interest rate.

10. Bonds are traded in the _____ market, thus the _____ of the bond may change as the supply and demand for money fluctuates. The _____ paid on the bond remains the same, but the bond's _____ changes. Most bonds are issued at their _____ or par value, meaning that when issued, the _____ is frequently equal to the _____ rate.

11. The three U.S. commercial rating companies that rate an issuer's _____ are _____ Investors Service, _____ Corporation, and _____ Ratings. A(n) _____ indicates a low credit risk which further translates into a good chance of future payments. The highest-grade bonds are those rated _____. Bond issues assigned a rating in the top four categories are _____-grade bonds and issues rated below the top four categories are _____-grade bonds, or _____-yield bonds or _____ bonds.

12. Bonds can have option provisions or a(n) _____ option that gives the _____ and/or the _____ an option to take some action against the other party. The most common type of option in a bond issue is a(n) _____ provision. This provision gives the right to _____ the debt, either in full or only in part, before the maturity date. An issue may include a(n) _____ provision allowing the bondholder to change the bond's maturity. It allows the bondholder the right to _____ the issue back to the issuer at par value on certain dates. A(n) _____ bond gives the right to exchange the bond for common stock.

13. Two major theories used to explain the observed shapes of the _____ curve are the _____ theory (which includes the _____ expectations theory, the _____ theory, and the _____ theory) and the market _____ theory.

SHORT ANSWER QUESTIONS

Refer to Chapter 3, pages 49–80 in *Financial Management and Analysis*.

1. Explain the function of financial intermediaries.

2. Describe the different types and purposes of the different deposit institutions.

3. How do nondeposit financial institutions manage their financial assets?

4. What are the components of the interest rate and the factors affecting these components?

5. What is the relationship between Treasury spot rates and forward rates? Why are forward rates also called *hedgeable rates*?

6. What is the purpose of the term structure of interest rates?

Introduction to Derivatives

FILL IN THE BLANKS

Refer to Chapter 4, pages 83–104 in *Financial Management and Analysis*.

1. A(n) _____ contract requires a participant to either _____ or _____ something, also known as the _____, at a specified future date at a set price. The future price agreed upon is the _____ price. The specified date on which the transaction occurs is the _____ date.

2. The basic _____ function of futures markets is to offer prospects to _____ against the _____ of price movements. _____ contracts are formed by _____ and involve traditional _____ commodities, imported foodstuffs, and _____ commodities. Instruments-based futures contracts are classified as _____ index futures, _____ rate futures, and _____ futures.

3. _____ are associated with futures and provide several functions such as _____ that two parties will carry out a preagreed transaction. _____ risk is the risk that the other party will default on their obligation on the _____ date. Due to the use of a clearinghouse, worry is removed from the parties to a(n) _____ contract.

4. In a futures contract, the investor must _____ a(n) _____ dollar amount per contract that the exchange dictates. Called the _____ margin, it is required as deposit for the contract. The _____ of the futures contract _____ and the investor's _____ changes. Recording the _____ value of a position is called _____ a position to _____ or simply _____ to _____.

5. When investors assume market positions by _____ a futures contract, the investor is in a(n) _____ position. On the other hand, if the investor's opening position is the _____ of a futures contract, the investor is in a(n) _____ position. A futures contract's _____ will recognize a(n) _____ if the futures price _____; the futures contract's _____ will recognize a(n) _____ if the futures price _____.

6. The _____ of the option grants the _____ of the option the right to purchase from

or _____ to the writer an asset at a specified _____ within a specified _____ of time. The option price is also called the option _____. The price at which the asset is _____ is the strike price. The date after which an option is void is called the _____ date.

7. Options exercised at _____ time up to and including the _____ date are a(n) _____ option. Options exercised only at the _____ date are _____ options. An option that can be exercised _____ the expiration date but only on _____ dates is called a(n) _____ option.

8. The option price is a reflection of the option's _____ value. Any amount over intrinsic value is referred to as the _____ premium. The intrinsic value of an option is the _____ value of the option if it is _____ immediately.

9. In a(n) _____ the counterparties agree to exchange _____ payments. The _____ amount of the payments exchanged is based on the _____ amount. _____ typically used by _____ companies are _____ rate swaps, _____ swaps, and _____ swaps. A swap has the _____ and _____ profile of a package of _____ contracts.

10. A(n) _____ is an agreement whereby the _____ agrees to pay the _____ when a designated reference _____ a predetermined level. A(n) _____ is an agreement whereby the _____ agrees to pay the _____ when a designated reference is _____ than a predetermined level. The designated reference could be a specific _____ rate or a(n) _____ price. A(n) _____ is equivalent to a package of _____ options; a(n) _____ is equivalent to a package of _____ options.

SHORT ANSWER QUESTIONS

Refer to Chapter 4, pages 83–104 in *Financial Management and Analysis*.

1. What are derivatives instruments and why are they useful?

2. How are futures liquidated?

3. What are the differences between futures contracts and forward contracts?

4. What are the differences between options and futures contracts?

5. What is the interpretation of a swap?

PROBLEMS

Refer to Chapter 4, pages 83–104 in *Financial Management and Analysis*.

1. Alex and Adrienne take positions in a futures contract. Alex is the buyer of the futures contract and Adrienne is the seller of the futures contract. If the futures price is $100, what are the possible outcomes for the market participants if Asset X increases to $135? If Asset X decreases to $50?

2. Illustrate the characteristics of a call and a put option contract given the following information: Lydia buys an American call (put) option for $3 with the following terms: The underlying is one unit of Asset X with an exercise price of $75 and an expiration date of three months from now.

3. Illustrate the purchase of a call option on Asset X that expires in two months and has an exercise price of $40 and an option price of $2. What is the profit or loss for the investor who purchases this call option and holds it until its expiration date?

4. If the exercise price for a call option is $100 and the current asset price is $110, what is the intrinsic value? What is the intrinsic value for a put option with an exercise price of $100 and a current asset price of $90?

5. Explain how futures are used to manage risk for a farmer who grows corn and a canning company who buys the corn for processing and selling in grocery stores.

CHAPTER 5

Taxation

FILL IN THE BLANKS

Refer to Chapter 5, pages 107–122 in *Financial Management and Analysis.*

1. In the United States, _____ passes the tax _____ that comprises the _____. The _____, a part of the Treasury Department, _____ these laws, _____ the details, and _____ them. The _____ does this by _____ and _____ tax forms, _____ tax payments, _____ the law in its regulations, and providing _____ in some situations.

2. The U.S. _____ originated in _____ with a(n) _____ tax on corporate income but has since become very _____. The financial _____ cannot simply assume that the tax rate in existence _____ will be the same in the _____. The _____-tax _____ of a firm over time must take into consideration the _____ tax rates.

3. The _____ tax rate is the rate that _____ the tax _____ and is the rate at which the next _____ of income would be taxed. The _____ tax rate is the _____ of the tax _____ to the taxable income. A(n) _____ tax is one that levies a higher _____ tax rate on _____ incomes. A company's _____ or _____ decision is likely to affect _____ income, and hence cash flow, through the _____ tax rate.

4. Corporate income distributed to _____ as _____ is taxed _____, first as _____ income and then as _____ income, and then if the shareholder is another _____, it could be taxed a(n) _____ time. To minimize the chance of _____ or more taxation of the same income, the tax laws permit a(n) _____ deduction. This is when a corporate _____ of _____ may deduct a portion of its _____ income from its _____ income. The _____ deduction _____ the after-tax _____ of a corporation _____ in another corporation's stock.

5. The two methods of depreciation available to business taxpayers are a(n) _____ method and a(n) _____ method. A firm can select a method of _____ that is based on the expected _____ of _____ depreciation of its assets

and the _____ on reported _____. The current depreciation tax laws are the result of an ongoing trend to create more _____ in _____ methods among business _____ while at the same time simplifying the _____ and allowing _____ depreciation and _____ asset lives.

6. According to the tax law, a(n) _____ is specifically a(n) _____ gain that results when an asset is _____ for more than was _____ for it. Congress has traditionally granted special _____ for capital gains through _____ effective _____ rates.

7. _____ tax credit (_____) was intended to _____ investment spending by directly _____ the _____ income tax. _____ can be _____ at any time that _____ feels investment _____ needs to be stimulated. Whereas _____ and _____ both _____ taxes payable, a(n) _____ reduces taxable income and thus _____ reduces the taxes paid.

8. A(n) _____ is an excess of business _____ over business gross _____ in a tax year. The IRC allows businesses to carry _____ a net operating loss to _____ years and to carry _____ the loss to _____ years to _____ the

taxes payable for those years. The current tax law permits net operating losses of corporations to be carried _____ three years from the year of the loss and carried _____ for 15 years.

9. Countries typically tax resident corporations on _____ income, regardless of whether the _____ is repatriated. _____ corporations, that is, corporations whose corporate _____ and place of _____ are outside the country, are typically subject only to _____ taxes derived from within the country. The _____ rates vary significantly from country to country and some impose _____ tax or _____ tax rates. These countries are referred to as tax _____.

SHORT ANSWER QUESTIONS

Refer to Chapter 5, pages 107–122 in *Financial Management and Analysis*.

1. In the United States there are several kinds of taxes imposed. What are they and what is their purpose?

2. How does dividend income affect investors? How does dividend income affect the corporation?

3. What are the features of the modified accelerated cost recovery system (MACRS) and how is this different from the straight-line method?

4. Should financial analysts be concerned with taxes? Should financial analysts be concerned with depreciation?

PROBLEMS

Refer to Chapter 5, pages 107–122 in *Financial Management and Analysis*.

1. ABC Corporation purchased a new computer system for $56,000 in 2000. The computer is classified as a seven-year property. What is the depreciation allowance for each year if:

   a. Straight-line depreciation method is used?

b. MACRS depreciation method is used?

3. What is the depreciation tax shield for ABC Corporation in problem 1 if ABC uses the MACRS depreciation method and has a corporate tax rate of 30%?

4. DEF Incorporated had $4 million in taxable income from operations and another $500,000 in dividend income that qualified for an 80% dividends-received deduction. If the firm is taxed at a flat rate of 35%, what is its tax liability?

5. GHI Company had a loss of $2 million for 2002. Calculate the amount of refund of prior taxes GHI can receive and how much loss can be carried forward, assuming the carry back/carry over rule will be utilized. The firm had income and paid taxes in the four years prior of:

Year	Taxable Income	Taxes Paid (35% of Taxable Income)
1998	$3,000,000	$1,050,000
1999	700,000	245,000
2000	500,000	175,000
2001	250,000	87,500

Financial Statements

FILL IN THE BLANKS

Refer to Chapter 6, pages 125–144 in *Financial Management and Analysis.*

1. _____ statements are summaries of the _____, _____, and _____ activities of a business. They provide useful _____ to both _____ and _____ in making credit, investment, and other business decisions by allowing them to _____ a company's future _____ and therefore the _____ flows expected to result from those _____.

2. The accounting _____ in _____ statements are prepared by the firm's _____ according to a set of standards, referred to as _____ or _____. The _____ sheet, or statement of financial _____ or statement of financial _____, is a summary of the _____, _____, and _____ of a business at a particular point in time—usually the end of the firm's _____ year, thus reflecting _____ costs.

3. The _____ sheet contains _____—the
resources of the business enterprise, such as plant and equipment that are used to generate _____ benefits
such as cash _____; _____—obligations of the business and commitments to _____
in the form of future cash _____; and
_____, also called _____ equity or
_____ equity, reflecting _____ of the
firm that is not owed to creditors.

4. _____ are made up of _____ liabilities, _____ liabilities, and _____
taxes. Current liabilities are obligations that must be paid
within one _____ cycle or _____ year,
whichever is longer. _____ payable,
_____ expenses, _____ of long-term
debt, and _____ loans are current liabilities.
_____ liabilities are obligations that must be
paid over a period _____ one year. They include
_____, _____, _____ obli-
gations, and _____ obligations.

5. _____ is the owner's _____ in the company. For a corporation, ownership is represented by
_____ stock and _____ stock. Share-
holders' equity is also referred to as the _____ of
equity, as this is the value of _____ according to
the records in the accounting books. The book value of equity
is the _____ total of _____ earnings,
_____ stock, and (if applicable) _____

stock and it represents the equity interest of the corporation's owners, stated in terms of _____ costs.

6. _____ shareholders' equity is the product of the number of _____ shares outstanding and the par value of the _____; it is shown that way on the _____. The _____ of the equity belongs to the _____ shareholders. It consists of three parts: _____ stock outstanding (listed at par or at stated value), additional _____ capital, and _____ earnings.

7. A(n)_____ statement is a(n) _____ of the _____ and _____ of a business over a period of time, usually one month, three months, or one year. This statement also is referred to as the _____ and _____ statement and shows the results of the firm's _____ and _____ decisions during that time.

8. The statement of _____ is a summary over a period of time of a firm's _____ flows from _____, _____, and _____ activities. The firm's statement of _____ lists separately its _____ cash flows, _____ cash flows, and _____ cash flows. A firm that generates cash flows only by _____ off its _____ (obtaining cash flows from investments) or by _____ more _____ (obtaining

cash flows from financing) cannot keep that up for very long. For future prosperity the firm must be able to generate cash flows from its _____, which is the most complex of the three.

9. Cash flow from _____ is generally obtained _____. The computation of the cash flows from _____ and _____ activities is straightforward. The cash flow from (used for) _____ activities includes cash flow due to _____ in plant assets, the _____ of plant assets, _____ of other companies, and _____ of subsidiaries. The cash flow from (used for) _____ activities includes cash flows due to the _____ or _____ of common or preferred _____, the _____ or _____ of long-term _____ securities, and the _____ of common and preferred _____.

10. Additional information about _____ can be found in the statement of _____ equity, which is a breakdown of the amounts and changes in _____ accounts. This statement serves as a connecting link between the _____ sheet and the _____ statement, providing the _____ with more detail on changes in the individual _____ accounts. Whereas the _____ sheet provides information on the _____ of shares outstanding at a specific point in time, the statement of _____ provides more detail on any changes,

including shares issued to satisfy the _____ of stock _____ and _____ shares.

SHORT ANSWER QUESTIONS

Refer to Chapter 6, pages 125–144 in *Financial Management and Analysis.*

1. What are the assumptions under which financial statements are created, used, and interpreted?

2. Name and describe the two categories of assets.

3. Define and provide examples of intangible assets.

4. Describe and list the labeling treatment shares receive on the balance sheet.

5. Why is it important to analyze the statement of cash flows? What does it tell an investor?

PROBLEMS

Refer to Chapter 6, pages 125–144 in *Financial Management and Analysis.*

1. Complete the following balance sheet:

Cash	$15,000	Accounts payable	$34,000
Inventory	_____	Notes payable	3,000
Gross plant and equipment	50,000	Long-term debt	
Accumulated depreciation	_____	Common equity	_____
Net plant and equipment	32,500		12,000
Total assets	$75,000	Total liabilities and equity	$75,000

2. Construct a statement of cash flows given the following
   information:

   Common stock dividends are 40% of earnings available to
   common shareholders.
   Earnings before taxes are $45,000.
   Preferred stock dividends are $20,000.
   Taxes are 30% of earnings.

3. Construct a statement of cash flows given the following information:

$15,000 in new long-term debt is issued.
$45,000 of common stock is repurchased.
Common stock dividends are $10,000.
Current liabilities are decreased by $30,000.
Depreciation is $60,000.
Net income is $54,000.
Plant and equipment purchased during the period is $58,000.

CHAPTER 7

Mathematics of Finance

FILL IN THE BLANKS

Refer to Chapter 7, pages 147–187 in *Financial Management and Analysis.*

1. The _____ of money is used to equate _____ flows at _____ points in time. One dollar received in the _____ is not as _____ as a dollar received _____ becasue it could be _____ today and earn _____. The process of calculating what one dollar today will be worth in the future is called _____ while the reverse is _____.

2. The amount that you are willing to _____ today is the loan's _____ value. The amount that you _____ to be _____ at the end of the loan period is the loan's _____ value. Therefore, the _____ period's value is comprised of two parts: Future Value = _____ value + _____. The _____ is compensation for the _____ of funds for a specific period. It consists of

compensation for the _____ of _____ the money is borrowed and compensation for the _____ that the amount _____ will not be _____ exactly as set forth in the loan agreement.

3. The _____ valuation equation, FV = _____, is used to translate _____ values into _____ values and to translate _____ values into _____ values. It also can be algebraically manipulated to solve for the _____ rate and the number of _____ periods. This basic relationship includes _____ compounding—that is, _____ earnings on _____ already earned.

4. We can use _____ mathematics to value many different _____ of _____ flows, including _____, _____ due, and _____ annuities. Applying the tools to these different patterns of cash flows requires us to take care in specifying the _____ of the various cash flows. _____ containing _____ factors, _____ factors, _____ value _____ factors, and _____ value _____ factors can be used to reduce the computations involved in financial math.

5. When faced with a(n) _____ of _____ flows, we must value each _____ flow individually, and then _____ these individual values to arrive at the _____ value of the _____ value of the series. The work can be cut a bit shorter if these

cash flows are _____ and occur at _____ intervals of time.

6. Valuing a(n) _____ cash flow stream is just like valuing a(n) _____ annuity. The _____ annuity cash flow analysis assumes that cash flows occur at the _____ of each period. However, it is fairly common to receive _____ cash flows at the _____ of the period; this is called a(n) _____.

7. A(n) _____ annuity has a stream of cash flows of _____ amounts at regular periods starting at some time _____ the end of the first _____. With a(n) _____ annuity, the _____ value of the _____ annuity is determined and then _____ to a(n) _____ period.

SHORT ANSWER QUESTIONS

Refer to Chapter 7, pages 147–187 in *Financial Management and Analysis.*

1. Why is a dollar today worth less than a dollar some time in the future?

2. How are interest rates with different compounding periods compared? Is there a method of comparison that is preferred?

PROBLEMS

Refer to Chapter 7, pages 147–187 in *Financial Management and Analysis*.

1. Using a 7.5% compounded interest rate per period, calculate the future value of a $500 investment:

   a. One period into the future

   b. Five periods into the future

c. Ten periods into the future

4. Using a 7.5% compounded interest rate per period, calculate the present value of a $500 investment to be received:

a. One period into the future

b. Five periods into the future

c. Ten periods into the future

4. If Natalie deposits $1,000 in her savings account and earns 4.5% interest per year:

a. How much would she have after three years if she left the money in the account to earn compound interest?

b. How much interest has she earned?

    c. If she would have withdrawn the interest each year, how much total interest would she have earned?

4. What growth rate does Larry need to double his initial investment over a five-year period?

5. How long will it take Wendy's $4,000 investment, compounded at 5% annual interest, to earn an additional $2,000?

6. Randy wants to borrow money for some home improvements. He has received several different quotes. Bank A will charge him 14.5% compounded annually, Bank B will charge him 14% compounded monthly, and his best friend will charge him 13.75% compounded continuously. Which is the better deal?

7. A credit card company advertises that it charges 2.9% interest on unpaid balances per month. What is the APR and EAR for this advertised rate?

8. What is the future value at the end of the third period of the following series of end-of-period cash flows, using an interest rate of 10% compounded per period?

Period	End-of-Period Cash Flows
0	$150
1	$300
2	$225
3	$410

9. Suppose an investment promises to provide the following cash flows:

Year	End-of-Year Cash Flow
1	$2,500
2	$3,000
3	$5,000
4	-$2,500

If interest is compounded annually at 12%, what is the value of this investment at the end of Year 0?

10. Suppose that you have won the Georgia Lotto worth $48 million. Further suppose that the State of Georgia will pay you the winnings in 20 annual installments, starting immediately, of $2,400,000 each. If your opportunity cost is 10%, what is the value today of these 20 installments?

11. Faith is saving money to send her son to college. If he is ten years old now, how much must she deposit now, at 7%, so that when he turns 18 and goes to college, he will be able to withdraw $20,000 a year for four years to pay for his college tuition?

CHAPTER 8

Principles of Asset Valuation and Investment Returns

FILL IN THE BLANKS

Refer to Chapter 8, pages 195–208 in *Financial Management and Analysis.*

1. The _____ manager must decide whether a particular investment is _____ or _____. A(n) _____ investment will _____ shareholder wealth whereas a(n) _____ one _____. To decide whether an investment is _____ or _____, the manager must determine whether the _____ from the investment that are often expected in future periods will _____ the _____. To make the _____ investment decisions, the _____ manager also must consider the way the investment is _____.

2. The _____ rate or _____ rate for the future cash flows is used to _____ these future cash flows into a(n) _____ value. This _____ rate represents how much an investor is willing to

_____ today for the _____ to receive the future cash flow. Or, to put it another way, the discount rate is the rate of _____ the investor _____ on an investment, given the _____ he or she is willing to pay for its _____ future cash flow. Whether a(n) _____ future cash flow, a(n) _____ of level cash flows, a(n) _____ of cash flows having different amounts, or a(n) _____ series of cash flows, to determine its _____ value, knowledge of the _____ and _____ of the future cash flows, as well as the _____ rate that reflects the uncertainty of these cash flows are necessary.

3. If investors are risk _____ then they do not like _____. They will value an asset using a(n) _____ discount rate the more _____ they are about the future cash flows. _____ and _____ will continue to _____ and _____ until they have exhausted what they believe are all the _____ opportunities. When that happens, the assets are neither _____ or _____ priced. This point where buying and selling is in _____ is referred to as a market _____.

4. The _____ of an asset is determined by the investor with the _____ valuation of the asset. As long as an asset can be traded without any _____ in a market, _____ and _____ will determine its price. However, if

there are frictions to trading such as a(n) _____ on the quantity or high transaction _____, trading is inhibited and the asset's price will not reflect the _____ value.

5. There is a(n) _____ relation between the _____ of an asset and the _____ rate applied to future cash flows: the _____ this _____ rate, the _____ today's _____, and the _____ the _____ rate, the _____ today's _____.

6. A(n) _____ is the _____ an investor receives from an investment. It can be in the form of a(n) _____ the in the _____ of the asset through _____ or _____, a cash _____ from the investment, such as a(n) _____ or a(n) _____ payment, or _____ a cash _____ and a change in _____.

7. The _____ on an investment is also referred to as the _____. The most common way of reporting a(n) _____ or _____ is on a(n) _____ basis, expressed as the _____ annual return. Another name for this _____ is the _____ rate of return (_____). The _____ annual return on an investment is the

_____ average, not the _____ average because it ignores any _____.

8. The _____ rate that equates an investment's initial _____ with value of the _____ cash flows it produces is the _____ rate of return. The _____ rate of return is aptly named as we are assuming that the cash _____ are reinvested at the _____ return as the rest of the investment, its _____ return.

9. The _____ annual return on an investment considers _____. If we assume the cash flows are _____ at a(n) _____ return, the return on the investment is referred to as the _____ rate of return (_____).

SHORT ANSWER QUESTIONS

Refer to Chapter 8, pages 195–208 in *Financial Management and Analysis*.

1. Why is there an inverse relation between the discount rate applied to future cash flows from an investment and the value of the investment today?

2. When given a choice among investments, on which aspects of the investments should the investor focus in order to make the best decision?

3. What are the differences among the average annual return, the arithmetic average annual return, and the geometric average annual return? Which one is preferred and why?

PROBLEMS

Refer to Chapter 8, pages 195–208 in *Financial Management and Analysis*.

1. Numerically illustrate the answer to short answer 1 from the section above, using the following information. Suppose Karen wants to make an investment today that will have a future value of $500 one year from today. If she has the choice of a 5% discount rate or a 6% discount rate, which investment should she choose?

2. A particular investment will pay $1,500 every year, forever. How much is this investment worth to an investor whose required rate of return is 10% for investments of similar risk?

3. Calculate the average annual return for a $3,000 investment with an ending price of $5,500 four years later, with no intermediate cash flows.

4. Consider an investment with the following cash flows:

Year	Cash Flows
2003	$20,000
2004	$40,000
2005	$25,000
2006	$35,000

a. What is the annual return on the investment if an investor invests $100,000 at the end of 2002?

b. What is the most the investor would invest so that the return on the investment is at least 10%?

3. Suppose $25,000 is invested and it provides a return of 8% in the first year, 12% in the second year, and 15% in the third year. The value of the investment is maintained in the investment and it grows each year (i.e., the investment has no cash flows).

   a. What is the investment worth at the end of the third year?

   b. What is the average annual return on this investment?

CHAPTER 9

Valuation of Securities and Options

FILL IN THE BLANKS

Refer to Chapter 9, pages 211–251 in *Financial Management and Analysis*.

1. Investing in _____ stock represents a(n) _____ interest in a corporation. _____ of common stock are a(n) _____ security meaning there is no _____. _____ of common stock have the _____ to receive a certain portion of any _____, however dividends are not _____. Typically _____ are either _____ or grow at a somewhat _____ rate.

2. _____ and _____ are debt securities obligating the borrower to pay _____ at regular intervals, typically _____, and to repay the _____ amount borrowed, referred to as the _____ value. The interest payment is called _____. If these coupons are a(n)

_____ amount, paid at regular intervals, we refer to the security paying them as having a(n) _____ coupon. A(n) _____-coupon note or bond does not promise to pay interest periodically; instead it pays only at the _____ date.

3. The _____ Model (_____) is a formula that can be used to _____ a share of _____ if the _____ is either _____ or grows at a(n) _____ rate. The model states that the _____ of a(n) _____ of stock is equal to the ratio of next period's _____ to the _____ between the _____ rate of _____ and the _____ rate of _____. Using the DVM, the _____ rate of _____ on a(n) _____ is a function of the stock's _____ yield and its _____ yield. Using the same model, the _____ rate is a function of the _____ payout such that the _____ the payout, the _____ the growth of future dividends and vice versa; the _____ the payout, the _____ it has to _____ into the firm for the future and the _____ the expected growth rate in the future.

4. If _____ are _____ forever, the _____ of a share of stock is the _____ value of the _____ per share per _____, in _____. The _____ rate of

_____ (_____) is the return share-holders demand to _____ them for the _____ of money tied up in their investment and the _____ of the _____ cash _____ from these investments.

5. _____ cost is what investors could have _____ on _____ investments with _____ risk. This _____ return is the _____ rate of _____, or the _____ rate, compensating the share owners for the _____ of money and _____. The required rate of return is made up of the _____ yield plus the rate the share _____ is expected to _____, the _____ yield. It becomes important to consider whether or not we actually realize the _____ yield only when we are dealing with _____ because _____ must be paid on the _____ gain only when it is _____.

6. When valuing _____, the present _____ is dependent on the relation between the _____ rate and the _____. If the _____ rate is more than the _____, the security is worth _____ than its _____ value and it sells at a(n) _____. If the _____ rate is less than the _____, the security is worth _____ than its maturity value and it sells at a(n) _____. If the _____ rate is equal to

the yield, the security is _____ at its maturity value.

7. A stock option is the _____ to _____ or _____ a particular common stock at a specified price within a specified period. These options are _____ created by the company that issued the underlying _____; rather, they are created by the _____ on which the option is to be _____. The right to _____ an asset is a(n) _____ option. It gives the investor the right to _____ a share of stock at the _____ price, or _____ price, before the _____ date. The right to _____ an asset is called a(n) _____ option.

8. A(n) _____ bond is a bond that can be converted into common _____ at the option of the _____. This bond is therefore a combination of a(n) _____ bond, a bond _____ such a conversion feature, and an option to convert the bond to shares of _____. _____ bonds have a call feature that allows the bond _____ to _____ back the bonds from the _____ at a specified _____, the _____ price, during a specified period _____ the bond's maturity date. Some bonds are both _____ and _____.

SHORT ANSWER QUESTIONS

Refer to Chapter 9, pages 211–251 in *Financial Management and Analysis.*

1. What is the relation between present value, maturity value, and selling price of a bond?

2. How are common stock, preferred stock, and debt securities valued?

3. What factors affect the time value of an option?

4. What is the Dividend Valuation Model and why is it useful for valuation purposes?

5. Compare the yield-to-maturity and yield-to-call for a bond.

PROBLEMS

Refer to Chapter 9, pages 211–251 in *Financial Management and Analysis.*

1. A bond has a coupon rate of 10%. Interest rates are expected to decrease due to a newly instituted economic package. What will happen to the price of this bond? Why?

2. A call option for 1,000 shares of XYZ Company is selling for $1,500. The option has a strike price of $30 and expires in one month. If a share of XYZ stock is currently selling for $32, does the cost of this option make sense? Why or why not?

3. ABC Corporation issues shares of preferred stock that sell for $35.00 and pays a fixed dividend of $3.45 a share. What is the annual return on the stock? If you require a 10% return on your investment, would you make this investment?

4. A share of HIJ preferred stock pays an $11.00 dividend and is priced to yield 8%. If the stock is callable at $125 in three years, and is currently priced at $130, should you take this investment?

5. The stock of NOP Corporation is currently paying a dividend of $2.25. The dividends are expected to grow at 2% for the next three years, after which the dividend is expected to remain at that level indefinitely. If investors require a 16% return on the stock, at what price should they sell?

6. An issue of bonds with a $1,000 face value paying a 12% coupon rate will mature in five years. Similar risk investments have an effective yield of 14% interest paid semiannually. At what price will the bonds be selling? If an investor bought a bond for the indicated price and held it to maturity, what would his average annual promised yield be?

7. An issue of JRJ Nibasco bonds pays a 9⅜% coupon and sold for 100 at the end of the year. If the bond sold for 103¾ at the end of the year, what return would an investor have earned for the year? What is the capital yield and the coupon yield on the bond?

8. What is the yield to maturity of an issue of zero-coupon bonds that mature in eight years and are selling for $63⅞?

9. An investor bought 1,000 shares of stock for $5 a share in her online trading account. The transaction cost for her was $10.99. One week later, she sold the shares for $8⅝, again incurring a $10.99 fee. The investor did not keep the investment long enough to qualify to receive any dividends from the company. What was her return on this investment?

10. A $1,000 bond of Needs-A-Name Corporation pays a 10% coupon and is selling for $108. The bond pays interest semiannually and is callable in four years at par plus one year's interest. What is its yield to call?

CHAPTER 10

Risk and Expected Return

FILL IN THE BLANKS

Refer to Chapter 10, pages 257–302 in *Financial Management And Analysis.*

1. There is _____ in almost everything financial managers do because no one _____ precisely what changes will occur in such things as _____ laws, consumer _____, the _____, or _____ rates. Though the terms _____ and _____ are often used to mean the same thing, there is a distinction between them. _____ is the lack of _____ what will happen in the future. _____ is how we characterize the degree of _____: the _____ the _____, the _____ the _____.

2. _____ flow risk comprises _____ risk, _____ risk, and _____ risk. _____ risk is the degree of _____ regarding the number of _____ of a(n)

_____ or service the firm will be able to sell and
the _____ of these units. _____ risk is
the uncertainty arising from the mix of _____
and _____ operating costs. _____ risk
is the uncertainty arising from the firm's _____
decisions.

3. The more burdened a firm is with _____,
required _____ and _____ payments,
the more likely it is that _____ promised to
_____ will not be made and that there will be
nothing left for the _____. We refer to the
_____ flow risk of a(n) _____ security
as _____ risk or _____ risk. Technically, _____ risk on a(n) _____ security
depends on the specific obligations comprising the debt.

4. _____ rate risk is the uncertainty associated
with _____ cash flows. If _____ fall,
one cannot _____ the _____ payments from the _____ and get the same
_____ as before. Of two bonds with the same
_____-to-maturity and the same _____
rate, the bond with the _____ maturity has
_____ reinvestment risk as it has _____
cash flows to _____ throughout its life. Likewise, of two bonds with the same _____-to-
maturity and the same _____ to _____,
the bond with the _____ coupon rate has
_____ reinvestment rate risk because it has

more of its _____ coming sooner in the form of cash flows.

5. _____ rate risk is the _____ of the change in an asset's _____ to changes in market _____ rates. _____ interest rates determine the _____ used to _____ a future value to a(n) _____ value, therefore the value of any investment depends on the rate used to _____ its cash flows to the present.

6. _____ power risk is the risk that the _____ may increase unexpectedly. For example, if a firm _____ funds by issuing a(n) _____-term bond with a fixed _____ rate and the price level _____, the firm _____ from a(n) _____ in the price level and its _____ is harmed because interest and the principal are repaid in a(n) _____ currency.

7. _____ risk is the risk that the relative values of the _____ and _____ currencies will change in the future, changing the _____ of the _____ cash flows. _____ risk must be considered when investments generate _____ flows in another _____.

8. _____ aversion is the _____ and avoidance of risk. A risk _____ investor will

_____ risky investments. Risk _____ indicates indifference towards risk. Risk _____ persons do not need _____ for bearing _____. Risk _____ indicates a(n) _____ for risk—someone who is even willing to pay to take on risk.

9. _____ is the combination of assets whose returns do not _____ with one another in the _____ direction at the _____ time. If the _____ on investments move together, they are _____ with one another. Correlation is the _____ for two or more sets of data to vary together. The _____ on two investments are _____ correlated if one tends to vary in the _____ direction at the same time as the other, and _____ correlated if one tends to vary in the _____ direction with respect to the other. They are _____ if there is _____ relation between the changes in one to changes in the other.

10. _____ that goes away as we _____ assets is diversifiable risk; this is also referred to as _____ risk or _____-specific risk. _____ that cannot be reduced by adding more _____ is nondiversifiable risk, also referred to as _____ risk or _____ risk.

11. _____ took the idea that portfolio _____ and _____ are the only elements to consider and developed a model that deals with how _____ are priced. This model is referred to as the _____ asset _____ model (_____). The _____ specifies that the _____ on any _____ is a function of the _____ on a(n) _____ asset plus a(n) _____ premium. The _____ on the risk-free asset is _____ for the time _____ of money. The risk _____ is the _____ for bearing _____. Therefore CAPM says: The market portfolio represents the most well _____ portfolio with the only _____ in a portfolio comprising all _____ being _____ risk, also called _____ risk or _____ risk.

12. An alternative to _____ in relating _____ and _____ is the _____ pricing _____ (_____), which was developed by _____. The _____ is a(n) _____ pricing model that is based on the idea that _____ assets in _____ markets should be priced _____. APM states that an asset's _____ should _____ the investor for the _____ of the asset, where the _____ is due to a number of _____ influences, or _____ factors. The APM provides _____ support for an asset _____ model where there is more than one risk _____.

SHORT ANSWER QUESTIONS

Refer to Chapter 10, pages 257–302 in *Financial Management and Analysis*.

1. What are the degree of operating leverage, the degree of financial leverage, and the degree of total leverage? How do they interact?

2. What may cause default and why should financial managers be concerned with default?

3. What two risks are closely associated with reinvestment risk? How do these risks contribute to reinvestment risk for the investor?

4. How does interest rate risk affect the valuation of bonds?

5. Explain the relationships among expected return, variance, and standard deviation.

PROBLEMS

Refer to Chapter 10, pages 257–302 in *Financial Management and Analysis*.

1. Home Decor Incorporated sells faux fur wallpaper for $1,500 per roll. The rolls cost the firm $30 to produce. The firm has fixed operating costs of $175,000 and pays an annual interest expense on its debt of $65,000.

   a. Calculate Home Decor's degree of operating leverage at 10,000 units sold.

b. Calculate Home Decor's degree of financial leverage at 10,000 units sold.

c. Calculate Home Decor's degree of total leverage at 10,000 units sold.

d. Calculate Home Decor's break-even number of units produced and sold.

e. If the sales volume were increased from 10,000 units to 15,000 units, by what percentage would the cash flow to shareholders increase?

6. Consider two investments with the following cash flows:

Economic Scenario	Probability of Economic Scenario	Possible Outcome for Investment 1	Possible Outcome for Investment 2
Boom	25%	$2,000	$1,500
Normal	40%	$1,000	$1,000
Bust	35%	$500	$857

a. Calculate the expected value of each investment.

b. Calculate the standard deviation for each investment's possible outcomes.

c. Which investment is riskier?

4. Suppose the expected risk-free asset is 6% and the return on the market is 10%. Further suppose you have a portfolio comprised of the following securities with equal investments in each:

Security	Security Beta
A	0.85
B	1.00
C	1.25
D	1.50

a. What is the expected return for each security in the portfolio?

b. What is the portfolio's beta?

c. What is the expected return on the portfolio?

4. Given the following investments:

Economic Scenario	Probability of Economic Scenario	Possible Outcome for Investment 1	Possible Outcome for Investment 2
Boom	15%	18%	25%
Normal	30%	50%	45%
Bust	55%	40%	30%

a. Calculate the covariance between the two investments.

b. Calculate the correlation coefficient between the two investments.

c. What do these measures tell an investor?

CHAPTER 11

The Cost of Capital

FILL IN THE BLANKS

Refer to Chapter 11, pages 307–347 in *Financial Management and Analysis.*

1. The _____ of _____ is the return that must be provided for the use of an investor's _____. If the funds are _____, the _____ is related to the _____ that must be paid on the loan. If the funds are _____, the _____ is the _____ that investors expect, both from the stock's price _____ and _____. The cost of _____ is the same as the _____ rate of _____.

2. Capital _____ is the mix of _____, _____ stock, and _____ stock. It is the goal of the financial manager to estimate the _____ of each in order for the firm to issue new _____.

3. The _____ of _____, which is the raising of one more _____ by issuing debt, is directly
affected by the _____ tax _____,
which provides the _____ rate on the next dollar
of _____ income. Because _____ paid is
deducted from _____ income, the _____
cost of debt is _____ than the stated cost.

4. When _____ securities and _____ are
issued, _____ costs must be considered. These costs
are _____ to _____, _____,
and investment _____ who assist the firm in the
issue. Also called _____ of debt, it drives
_____ the cost of the issue.

5. The _____ of _____ stock is the cost
associated with raising one more _____ of capital by _____ shares of _____ stock.
_____ stock may or may not have a(n)
_____. If it does not have a(n) _____,
then it is called _____ stock.

6. The _____ of _____ stock is the cost
of raising one more dollar of _____ equity
capital, either _____ or _____.
_____ generated capital comes from
_____ earnings whereas _____ generated capital comes from issuing new _____
of _____ stock.

7. The _____ Model (_____) for valuing _____ stock states the _____ of a share of _____ is the _____ value of all its _____ cash _____ that are _____ at the _____ rate of _____ on _____. It is based on the assumption that _____ grow at a(n) _____ rate into the _____.

8. The _____ Model (_____) assumes investors hold _____ portfolios that are only subject to _____ risk. Investors are _____ for the _____ value of _____ and for the _____ they assume. The _____ for the _____ value of _____ is represented by the market _____ and the riskiness of the _____ is represented by _____.

9. The _____ budget implies that in order to _____ shareholder wealth, _____ in projects must be made until the _____ cost of _____ is _____ to its marginal _____. In other words, the _____ is the capital _____ where the _____ cost of _____ intersects the _____ rate of return, also known as the marginal _____ of capital.

SHORT ANSWER QUESTIONS

Refer to Chapter 11, pages 307–347 in *Financial Management and Analysis*.

1. Explain what is meant when it is said that the cost of capital and the required rate of return are marginal concepts.

2. How is the cost of capital determined?

3. Under what financial conditions is it appropriate to use the DVM? The CAPM?

PROBLEMS

Refer to Chapter 11, pages 307–347 in *Financial Management and Analysis*.

1. Tallahassee Trucking and Towing (TTT) wants to issue additional debt. Using the yield on their current debt as a guide for the cost of new debt, what is TTT's after-tax cost of debt? They currently have a 7% coupon bond paying interest semiannually that matures in five years and it has a current market price of $90 or $900 per $1,000 face value bond.

2. H&H, Inc., estimates they can sell an issue of $35 par value preferred stock that has a dividend rate of 3% to be paid at the end of each year. What is the all-in-cost of preferred stock if they sell the issue at par value with no flotation costs? With flotation costs of 1% of par value?

3. Rose Flower Company is considering issuing new stock. The current stock price is $65 per share and the corresponding current dividend of $3.12 per share and the dividends are expected to grow at a rate of 5% per year. Using the Dividend Valuation Model, what is the cost of common stock?

4. ABC Company is considering issuing new stock and is evaluating its cost of equity capital. If the risk-free rate of interest is 4% and the return on the market is 11%, what is the cost of common stock using the Capital Asset Pricing Model, assuming ABC has a beta of 1.35?

5. Sutton, Inc., is evaluating its cost of capital under alternative financing arrangements. It expects to be able to issue new debt at par with a coupon rate of 8% and to issue new preferred stock with a $2.00 per share dividend at $30 a share. The common stock is currently selling for $25 a share. It expects to pay a dividend of $1.50 per share next year. Sutton expects dividends to grow at a rate of 5% per year and Sutton's marginal tax rate is 40%. Consider the two arrangements that follow to answer this question: What is the cost of capital to Sutton, Inc., under each financing arrangement?

Financing	Percentage of New Capital Raised		
Arrangement	Debt	Preferred Stock	Common Stock
1	30%	10%	60%
2	50%	25%	25%

Capital Budgeting: Cash Flows

FILL IN THE BLANKS

Refer to Chapter 12, pages 355–392 in *Financial Management and Analysis.*

1. The financial manager's _____ is to maximize owners' _____. To accomplish this, the manager must evaluate _____ opportunities and determine which ones will add _____ to the firm. Firms continually _____ funds in _____ and _____ assets and these assets produce _____ and _____ flows that the firm can then either _____ in more assets or _____ to the owners.

2. _____ investment is the firm's investment in its _____ through the use of _____, _____, _____, and _____ financing. The firm's _____ investment decision may be comprised of a number of distinct _____. Managers must evaluate a number of

_____ in making investment decisions, not only to _____ how much the firm's _____ cash flows will _____ if it invests in a project, but also the _____ associated with these _____ cash flows.

3. Cash flow _____ comes from two sources: _____ risk and _____ risk. _____ risk is the degree of _____ related to the number of units that will be _____ and the _____ of the good or service and _____ risk is the degree of _____ concerning _____ cash flows that arises from the particular _____ of fixed and variable _____ costs. The combination of the two risks is _____ risk and is reflected in the _____ rate, which is the rate of _____ required to compensate the suppliers of _____ for the amount of risk they bear, the _____ rate of return or, from the firm's perspective, the _____ of capital.

4. Capital _____ is the process of _____ and _____ investments in _____ lived assets, or assets expected to produce _____ over more than _____ year. Because a firm must continually evaluate possible investments, capital _____ is a(n) _____ process. However, before a firm begins thinking about capital _____, it must first determine its corporate _____ —its broad set of _____ for future investment.

5. Projects are classified by the _____ of the project life, the _____, and the _____ on other projects. The _____ or _____ life of an asset is an estimate of the _____ of time that the asset will provide _____ to the firm. The investment's _____ of return can be classified according to the _____ of the project represented by the investment. The degree of _____ on other projects is classified as follows: _____ projects, _____ projects, _____ projects, and _____ projects.

6. The _____ between the cash flows of the firm _____ the investment project and the cash flows of the firm _____ the investment project, both over the same period of time, is the project's _____ cash flows. A more useful way of evaluating the _____ in the value is the breakdown of the project's cash flows into two _____: _____ cash flows and _____ cash flows, which are the _____ needed to _____ the project's assets and any cash flows from _____ of the project's assets.

7. The _____ form of investment is a cash _____ when the asset is _____ and there may be either a cash _____ or a(n) _____ at the end of its _____ life. In most cases these are not the only cash flows—the investment may result in changes in _____, _____, _____, and _____

capital. These are _____ cash flows as they result directly from the day-to-day activities of the firm.

8. The effect _____ has on taxes is called the _____. Because it reduces taxable income, depreciation reduces the tax _____, which amounts to a cash _____. For tax purposes, firms are permitted to use _____ depreciation or _____ depreciation. A(n) _____ method is preferred in most situations because it results in _____ deductions _____ in the asset's life than using _____ depreciation.

9. _____ value is _____ considered in calculating _____. Instead, it is our best _____ today of what the _____ will be _____ at the end of its _____ life some time in the future. _____ value is our estimate of how much we can get when we _____ of the asset.

SHORT ANSWER QUESTIONS

Refer to Chapter 12, pages 355–392 in *Financial Management and Analysis*.

1. List and describe the five stages of the capital budgeting process.

2. Compare the investment decisions in short-term assets versus long-term assets.

3. Explain the difference between independent, mutually exclusive, contingent, and complementary projects.

4. What are the cash flows that comprise an investment?

PROBLEMS

Refer to Chapter 12, pages 355–392 in *Financial Management and Analysis*.

1. An asset is purchased for $10,000. It is classified as five-year property and will be depreciated using the straight-line method. The asset has no salvage value and is

expected to increase revenues by $15,000 a year and expenses by $8,000 a year. If the tax rate is 30%, determine the cash flows from asset acquisition, asset disposition, and operating cash flows.

2. The Cookies-R-Us bakery is considering the purchase of an additional cookie press for $49,000. It is classified as a seven-year property and will be depreciated using straight-line depreciation. The addition of the press is expected to increase revenues by $18,000 a year and cash operating expenses by $5,000 a year. The salvage value is $10,000 at the end of seven years. If the tax rate is 25%, determine the cash flows from asset acquisition, asset disposition, and operating cash flows.

3. A new piece of equipment will cost a firm $20,000 to purchase and $8,000 to install and make it adaptable to the firm's specific needs. In addition, $2,000 investment in spare parts inventory will be maintained to prevent downtime. The equipment has a seven-year life and will be depreciated using the straight-line method. It is expected to have a salvage value of $5,000 at the end of seven years. It will have no effect on revenues but is expected to decrease expenses by $3,000 a year through cost efficiencies. Determine the cash flows from asset acquisition, asset disposition, and operating cash flows.

CHAPTER 13

Capital Budgeting Techniques

FILL IN THE BLANKS

Refer to Chapter 13, pages 399–444 in *Financial Management and Analysis.*

1. The _____ of capital is what the firm must _____ for the funds needed to _____ an investment. The _____ of capital may be a(n) _____ cost, such as the _____ paid on debt, or a(n) _____ cost, such as the expected _____ appreciation of shares of the firm's _____ stock, or the _____ required by the _____ of _____ to compensate them for the time _____ of money and the _____ associated with the investment. The more _____ the future cash flows, the _____ the cost of capital.

2. The _____ period for a project is the _____ of time it takes to get your _____ back. It is the period from the _____ cash _____ to the

time when the project's cash _____ add up to the
_____ cash _____. The _____
period is also referred to as the _____ period or the
capital _____ period.

3. The _____ period is the time needed to
_____ back the _____ investment in
terms of _____ future cash flows, therefore the
_____ period is _____ for
_____ cash flows than for _____
flows that are not _____.

4. The _____ value (_____) is the
present value of all _____ cash flows. The
term _____ is used because we want to determine the _____ between the _____
in the operating cash flows and the investment cash
flows. Often _____ in operating cash flows are
_____ and the _____ cash flows are
_____, hence the reference to the
_____ as the _____ between the
present value of the cash _____ and the
present value of the cash _____.

5. The _____ technique considers all expected
_____ cash flows, the _____ of
money and the _____ of the _____
cash flows. Evaluating projects using _____ will
lead us to select the ones that _____ owners'

wealth. The _____ technique also allows you to _____ the effect of _____ in cost of capital on a project's _____.

6. A project's _____ profile, also referred to as the _____ profile, shows how _____ changes as the _____ rate changes. The _____ profile is a(n) _____ depiction of the relation between the _____ of a project and the _____ rate. It shows the _____ of a project for a(n) _____ of _____ rates.

7. The _____ (_____) is the ratio of the present value of change in _____ cash _____ to the present value of _____ cash _____. The _____ is often referred to as the _____ ratio, as it is the ratio of the _____ from an investment to its _____. The _____ tells us how much value we get for each dollar invested.

8. An investment's _____ of return (_____) is the _____ rate that makes the present value of all expected _____ cash flows equal to _____; or, in other words, the _____ is the _____ rate that causes _____ to equal _____. The _____ is a(n) _____—what is earned, on average, per year. When evaluating _____

projects, the one with the highest _____ may _____ be the one with the best NPV.

SHORT ANSWER QUESTIONS

Refer to Chapter 13, pages 399–444 in *Financial Management and Analysis*.

1. What are the six capital budgeting techniques? What should be taken into consideration when applying each technique?

2. What are the decision criteria for each capital budgeting technique?

3. When should PI be used? When should it not be used?

4. What is the difference between the IRR and MIRR? Why is using IRR or MIRR sometimes not appropriate?

5. Of all the capital budgeting techniques, which one is the best evaluation technique? Which techniques do managers most prefer in practice?

PROBLEMS

Refer to Chapter 13, pages 399–444 in *Financial Management and Analysis*.

1. You are the manager and are considering the following two projects for investment:

	Year 0	Year 1	Year 2	Year 3
Project A	($10,000)	$3,000	$7,000	$9,000
Project B	($5,000)	$3,000	$4,000	$5,000

a. Calculate the payback period assuming end-of-the-year cash flows.

b. Calculate the discounted payback period assuming a required rate of return of 10% and end-of-the-year cash flows.

c. Calculate the NPV of each project.

d. Calculate the PI of each project.

e. Calculate the IRR of each project.

f. Calculate the MIRR of each project assuming a reinvestment rate of 10%.

g. If the projects are independent, which should be undertaken?

h. If the projects are mutually exclusive, which one should be undertaken?

CHAPTER 14

Capital Budgeting and Risk

FILL IN THE BLANKS

Refer to Chapter 14, pages 451–481 in *Financial Management and Analysis.*

1. Uncertainty arises from different sources, depending on the type of _____ being considered, as well as the circumstances and the _____ in which it is operating. Such circumstances include _____ conditions, _____ conditions, _____, _____ rates, and _____ conditions.

2. The sources of _____ influence _____ cash flows when _____ the risk of a capital project. Therefore, there is a(n) _____ cost to consider: what the suppliers of capital could _____ elsewhere for the _____ level of _____. This is the required _____ or cost of _____ and it contains the _____ return necessary to _____ investors for the risk they bear, called the _____ premium.

3. A project's _____ in isolation from the firm's other _____ is also referred to as the project's _____ risk or _____ risk. Because most firms have many _____, the _____ risk of a project under consideration may not be the _____ risk for analysis. A firm is a(n) _____ of assets, and the _____ of these different assets are not perfectly, positively _____ with one another. The real concern is with the _____ of the project to the firm's _____ of assets and how it changes the _____ of the firm's _____.

4. Three _____ measures are used to evaluate the _____ associated with a(n) _____ possible outcomes: the _____, the _____ _____, and the _____ of _____. The more _____ or spread out the possible outcomes, the _____ the degree of _____ or risk of what is expected in the future.

5. In attempting to asses risk, it is important to perform analyses of the _____ of cash flows to _____ in the assumptions by _____ the cash flows for different _____. _____ analysis, also called _____ analysis or _____ analysis, is a method of looking at the possible _____, given a change in only _____ of the factors at a time.

6. _____ analysis provides a manageable approach to changing _____ or _____ factors at the _____ time. It is _____ simulation by developing a(n) _____ distribution of possible _____, given a(n) _____ distribution for each _____ that may _____. With the help of a computer simulation program, _____ can be performed calculating _____ of return that yield a(n) _____ distribution of the _____ on investments.

7. An alternative approach that applies _____ methods to _____ assets, known as _____ valuation (_____), considers the value of a project that extends _____ its value as measured by the _____, meaning the value of project is _____ by the value of _____ inherent in an investment opportunity. These _____ are to _____ the project, though there may be constraints (e.g., legally binding contracts) that affect when this option can be _____, the option to _____, and the option to _____ investment to some _____ date. Because the options are _____ decisions, the _____ net present value is referred to as the _____ NPV.

8. The _____ of stock options is rather complex, but with the assistance of models such as the _____ model, option values can be estimated. The _____ option pricing model contains _____ factors that

are important in the _____ of an option. The most _____ and _____ factor to measure, the _____ of the value of the underlying asset, directly affects _____ key elements of the _____ value in that the greater the _____, the greater the _____ of the option and the greater the _____ of _____, which lowers the _____ NPV.

9. A(n) _____ equivalent is the _____ cash flow that is considered to be _____ to the _____ cash flow. The _____ equivalent _____ of incorporating _____ into the net present value analysis is useful because it _____ the time _____ of money and _____, allows each _____ cash flows to be adjusted separately for _____, and _____ for risk can be _____. It is difficult to apply as the _____ value of the certainty equivalent is not easily _____ and there is no _____ way of determining the certainty equivalent value for each _____ cash flow.

10. Considering the use of a(n) _____ cost of _____ and/or similar _____ for all projects can be hazardous. When _____ the various _____ capital _____ techniques, it may result in the _____ of profitable projects that have risk below the risk of the average risk project because of _____ future cash flows, and

_____ of unprofitable projects whose risk is above the risk of the average project, because future cash flows were _____.

SHORT ANSWER QUESTIONS

Refer to Chapter 14, pages 451–481 in _Financial Management and Analysis_.

1. Define and explain how the range, standard deviation, and coefficient of variation are used to describe the dispersion of future outcomes.

2. What are sensitivity and simulation analyses and when are they appropriate?

3. How does financial leverage affect the measurement of market risk?

4. If a firm is considering engaging in a new project, how does it measure the risk for this new project?

5. How is a firm's cost of capital generally determined?

PROBLEMS

Refer to Chapter 14, pages 451–481 in *Financial Management and Analysis*.

1. ABC Company's cost of capital is 15% and uses equity financing. It is investigating the possibility of investing in a project that is different from its line of business. ABC has identified a pure play firm, DEF, Inc., for that particular project that has an equity beta of 1.36. DEF has a 45% debt to equity ratio and has a 35% marginal tax rate. What rate of return should ABC use to evaluate taking on the project if the relevant risk-free rate is 5.5% and the market risk premium is 12%?

2. Consider the following cash flows for Projects A and B.

Project A		Project B	
Probability	Cash Flow	Probability	Cash Flow
0.25	$1,300	0.30	$3,000
0.40	$1,500	0.25	–$1,000
0.35	$800	0.45	$1,500

a. What are the cash flows range for each project?

b. What is the expected cash flow for each project?

c. What is the standard deviation of the possible cash flows for each project?

d. What is the coefficient of variation for each project?

e. Assume a firm is trying to decide between these two projects and uses a 13% required rate of return to evaluate all the projects having a coefficient of variation of less than 0.5 and an 18% required rate for those projects with coefficients greater than 0.5. Project A requires an initial outlay of $2,000, whereas Project B costs $1,000. Each project is expected to have a five-year life. Which project should be undertaken if the projects are mutually exclusive?

f. Conduct a sensitivity analysis on Project B making each of the following changes:
  ■ Change the discount rate to 19%.

■ Change the initial outlay to $ 1,800.

■ Change the expected cash flows to $1,000.

■ Assume all these changes occur at the same time.

CHAPTER 15

Intermediate and Long-Term Debt

FILL IN THE BLANKS

Refer to Chapter 15, pages 487–527 in *Financial Management and Analysis*.

1. The amount borrowed in a(n) _____ is called the _____ and is repaid either at the _____ of the period or at regular _____ during this period. The _____ or note holder or _____ receives _____ as compensation. For some types of debt the _____ is paid periodically, and for other types is paid at the _____ of the debt period. The interest rate can be a(n) _____ rate or a(n) _____ rate which is popularly referred to as a(n) _____ rate.

2. Debt backed by _____ is called _____ debt and the property is _____ or _____. If there is no security, the creditor relies entirely on the _____ of the borrower to make

the promised _____; therefore this type of debt is _____ or a(n) _____.

3. _____ loans are negotiated directly between _____ and _____, where the _____ is typically a commercial _____, a(n) _____ company, or a(n) _____ company. _____ loans range in _____ from two to ten years, though any repayment term is possible as long as it is a(n) _____ term, or _____ maturity, as opposed to a loan that is payable on _____.

4. Bonds may be either _____ or _____. For _____ bonds, the issuer maintains _____ of who owns them and sends any _____ or _____ to the _____ owners. For _____ bonds, physical _____ of the _____ entities the receiver to the _____. If _____ is payable, the _____ simply clips a(n) _____ attached to the certificate and sends it in or _____ it at a specified bank.

5. The _____ feature of a convertible bond gives the investor the right to _____ the bond for some other _____, typically shares of _____, at a predetermined rate of exchange. The _____ should hold the bond until it becomes

_____ to convert it into shares of stock. It won't be worth converting unless the _____ of the shares of stock _____.

6. Organizations that _____ and _____ the likelihood of debt _____ and make the information available to the public are _____ agencies. The most popular agencies are _____ Service, _____ Corporation, and _____. The debt or _____ ratings are important for the _____ of and _____ of debt. Many banks, pension funds, and governmental bodies are _____ from investing in securities that do not have a(n) _____ credit rating. Because investors want to be compensated for _____, the _____ the _____ risk associated with debt, represented by _____ ratings, the _____ the yield on debt demanded by investors, which means the _____ the cost of raising funds via debt.

7. In all _____ systems, the term _____ grade means _____ default risk, or conversely, _____ probability of future payments. In general, _____ bonds carry the highest-grade or _____ ratings that are designated by a symbol of triple _____ through triple _____. _____ bonds are those bonds rated below triple _____ and are also called _____ or _____ or _____ bonds.

8. _____ agencies consider the four Cs of
   _____: _____, _____,
   _____, and _____. _____
   of management includes the _____ reputation
   and _____ of management. _____ is
   the ability of an issuer to _____ its obligations.
   Collateral is the _____ of _____ and
   _____ that are pledged to secure debt.
   _____ are the binding _____ and
   _____ of the lending agreement.

9. Firms seeking to raise _____ with
   _____ offerings want to issue securities with the
   _____ cost and the flexibility to _____
   the debt if interest rates _____. Investors want
   securities that provide the _____ yield,
   _____ risk, and the flexibility to _____
   if other, more profitable investment opportunities arise. The
   best package of _____ features will provide both
   what investors are looking for and what the firm is willing to
   offer. Today, this is available through the use of
   _____ instruments because issuers can
   _____ create _____-rate or
   _____-rate bonds by using _____ rate,
   _____, _____, or _____
   based swaps.

SHORT ANSWER QUESTIONS

Refer to Chapter 15, pages 487–527 in *Financial Management and Analysis.*

1. How is the interest rate on debt determined and how is it reset for floating rates?

2. Describe and discuss the difference between a fully amortizing loan and a bullet loan.

3. What is the difference between a note and a bond?

4. Describe the basic provisions of a bond issue.

5. How would a bond be called or retired prior to maturity? Why would this happen?

6. What is the difference between a convertible bond and a bond with a warrant option?

PROBLEMS

Refer to Chapter 15, pages 487–527 in *Financial Management and Analysis*.

1. Which would experience a greater percentage change in price if interest rates change and which has more reinvestment risk: an 8% coupon bond with 10 years to maturity or a zero-coupon bond with 10 years to maturity? Why?

2. TJ Corporation currently has a 9%, $1,000 bond issue outstanding. The bond is convertible into 45 shares of common stock and is currently selling for $1,575.

   a. What is the conversion price of the bond?

b. If the common stock is currently selling for $35 a share, what is the bond's market conversion price?

c. What is the effective conversion price of the bond?

d. The bond is callable at $1,800. Should an investor accept the call or convert the bond into common stock? Why?

3. CVQ Inc., has issued $100 million of 8% coupon bonds. Each has a warrant that entitles the owner to buy a share of the common stock of CVQ for $20 a share.

   a. If the current market price of CVQ is $33 a share, what is the minimum price you would pay for the warrant?

   b. The warrant has five years until expiration. How will this affect the price you would be willing to pay for the warrant?

4. KLH Company currently has $12 million of 10% coupon bonds outstanding. The bonds pay interest semiannually, they have a face value of $1,000 each, and have eight years remaining to maturity. The bonds are callable at 105 and are trading to yield 6%. KLH's marginal tax rate is 25%.

a. What is the total market value of the outstanding bonds?

b. Should KLH buy the bonds in the open market or call in the bonds at this point in time? Why?

5. The DD Corporation issued a zero-coupon, $1,000 face value bond on January 1, 2001. The bond was issued at $875 and matures on December 31, 2003.

   a. If you bought these bonds when they were issued and held them to maturity, what return would you earn?

   b. What is the amount of interest expense on this bond that DD can deduct each year?

CHAPTER 16

Common Stock

FILL IN THE BLANKS

Refer to Chapter 16, pages 533–566 in *Financial Management and Analysis.*

1. We refer to the equity of a corporation as _____. A corporation's stock may be divided into two major types: _____ stock and _____ stock. Each of these classes is split into smaller pieces called _____, represented by stock _____. Owners of these shares are referred to as _____ or _____. Shareholders receive part of the _____ on their investment from _____, which are periodic _____ payments from the corporation.

2. There are a number of characteristics of _____ stock that are important in the financial manager's capital structure decision and that affect investors' decisions regarding common stock as an investment. These characteristics include: limited _____, the number of

_____, stock _____, _____ stock, _____ rights, and the right to _____ more stock.

3. The number of _____ a firm can issue is referred to as the _____ shares. If a firm wishes to issue more shares, it does _____ have to issue the entire number of shares authorized. The number of _____ shares is the number of shares _____ sold and is equal to or _____ than the number of _____ shares. If a firm buys back stock from investors, the number of shares _____ in the hands of investors—referred to as _____ shares—is fewer than the number of _____ shares. Shares bought back from investors may be either _____, reducing the number of issued shares, or held as _____ stock.

4. _____ shareholders are generally granted rights to _____ members of the board of _____, _____ on the _____ of the corporation with another corporation, _____ additional shares of common stock, and _____ on _____ to the articles of incorporation. Different _____ of stock may have different numbers of _____ per share, or different classes as a whole may have specified _____ of the votes. The different classes can be used by _____ groups to _____ control of the company.

5. _____ voting is designed to allow _____ shareholders to gain representation on the board. With _____ voting, shareholders can _____ their votes for members of the board of directors. Cumulative voting allows shareholders to _____ up their votes for one or more _____, leading to more active participation in the corporation's _____, especially by shareholders with _____ holdings.

6. Some corporations have divided their director positions into classes, where only _____ class of directors is voted on each year, instead of the _____ board. This system is referred to as a(n) _____ board of directors or a(n) _____ board of directors. The _____ of this system is that, by staggering terms there is _____ in the board of directors. Having multiyear terms insures that there are _____ members of the board and allows the board as a group to work on projects or issues that extend beyond _____.

7. Corporations can give the right to buy _____ shares of new _____ stock through a(n) _____ offering which is an offering of _____ to _____ shareholders to purchase shares in order to _____ their current _____ in the company.

8. The board of _____ may declare a(n) _____ at any time, but dividends are not a legal _____ of the corporation. Most dividends are in the form of _____. In addition to cash dividends, the corporation may provide shareholders with dividends in the form of additional _____ of stock or, rarely, other types of _____ owned by the corporation.

9. Many U.S. corporations allow shareholders to automatically _____ their dividends in the _____ of the corporation paying them. A(n) _____ reinvestment plan (_____) is a program that allows _____ to reinvest their _____, buying _____ shares of stock of the company instead of receiving the _____ dividend. These _____ shares representing dividends reinvested may be currently _____ or newly _____.

10. A stock _____ is something like a stock dividend. A stock split _____ the number of _____ shares into _____ shares however the _____ of ownership has not changed. Aside from a minor difference in accounting, stock splits and stock dividends are essentially the _____. A(n) _____ stock split, _____ the price of a stock by _____ the number of shares of stock.

11. A(n) _____ policy is a firm's _____ about the payment of _____ dividends to shareholders. There are several basic ways of describing a firm's dividend policy: _____ dividends, constant _____ in dividends per share, constant _____ ratio, and _____ dividends with _____ extra dividends. Several views that attempt to explain why dividends are paid are: the Dividend _____ Theory, the "_____ in the Hand" Theory, the _____ Explanation, the _____ Explanation, and the _____ Explanation.

12. A corporation _____ its own shares is effectively paying a(n) _____ dividend, with one important difference: _____. _____ dividends are _____ taxable income to the shareholder. A firm's _____ of shares, on the other hand, results in a(n) _____ gain or loss for the shareholder, depending on the _____ paid when they were originally purchased. If the shares are repurchased at a(n) _____ price, the difference may be taxed as capital _____, which may be taxed at rates _____ than ordinary income.

SHORT ANSWER QUESTIONS

Refer to Chapter 16, pages 533–566 in *Financial Management and Analysis.*

1. Exactly what is a shareholder buying when shares are purchased?

2. What is the difference between preferred stock and common stock?

3. What is common equity and how is it created?

4. What does it mean when corporations are classified as publicly held, privately held, or closely held?

5. Why would a company pay a dividend?

6. Explain the time line for issuing dividends.

7. Why would a company do a reverse stock split?

8. Why would a company repurchase its own stock and how would it go about doing so?

PROBLEMS

Refer to Chapter 16, pages 533–566 in *Financial Management and Analysis*.

1. ABC Corporation has 1.3 million common shares outstanding and total earnings of $2.4 million. The firm paid dividends totaling $550,000. The firm has no preferred stock.

   a. What were the dividends per share paid by ABC?

   b. What was ABC's dividend payout ratio?

2. Pricee stock sells for $275 per share and you own 300 shares.

   a. What is the current market value of your investment?

   b. What is the new price per share, new amount of shares you will own, and the new market value of your investment if the firm declares a 3 for 1 stock split? If the firm declares a 15% stock dividend?

3. You currently own 500 shares of XYZ Company. There are four board positions up for election. How many votes can you cast for your favorite candidate, Ms. W, if the ordinary voting procedure is used? How many can you cast for Ms. W if cumulative voting is used?

CHAPTER 17

Preferred Stock

FILL IN THE BLANKS

Refer to Chapter 17, pages 571–580 in *Financial Management and Analysis.*

1. Like common stock, _____ stock also represents equity. _____ shareholders have a claim on _____ and assets ahead of that of _____ shareholders. If the business is liquidated and all the assets sold and the proceeds used to pay off all the creditors, then the _____ shareholders get what is owed to them before _____ shareholders. While few corporations are actually liquidated, this _____ claim provides _____ shareholders with an advantage in the reorganization of firms in distress or bankruptcy.

2. Almost all firms must pay their specified _____ dividend. When dividends are paid, _____ dividends must be paid _____; what remains may be paid as dividends to _____ shareholders. Most preferred share _____ are paid in _____,

although some are in the form of _____ of stock. Most _____ dividends are paid _____ and may be paid at either a(n) _____ or _____ rate per period.

3. _____ dividends are expressed as either a(n) _____ of the par value or a(n) _____ dollar amount per period. For _____ dividends, the dividend rate on a(n) _____ preferred stock is typically fixed _____ and based on the dividend _____ spread. Most adjustable-rate preferred stock is _____, with a(n) _____. From the perspective of the _____, a collar's maximum ensures that the _____ of financing with preferred stock are _____; from the perspective of the _____, a collar's minimum ensures that the _____ on the preferred stock has a(n) _____ limit.

4. The dividend rate on _____ preferred stock is set _____, as with adjustable-rate preferred stock, but it is established through an auction process. _____ preferred stock is preferred stock where the dividend rate is determined periodically by a remarketing _____ who resets the dividend rate so that any preferred stock can be _____ at par and be resold at the original _____ price. Typically, a(n) _____ has the choice of dividend _____ every seven days or every 49 days. Since the mid-1980s, _____ preferred stock and

_____ preferred stock have become the dominant type of preferred stock issued.

5. With _____ preferred stock, any _____ not paid in one period must be paid the next period _____ any other dividend for that class of preferred stock is paid and before any _____ stock dividend is paid. With _____ preferred stock, any dividend not paid in a period is _____ paid in any other period—it is simply _____ and does not affect the dividend in any _____ period. If a preferred stock dividend is _____, any dividend passed over in one period is carried over year to year. The passed over dividend is referred to as the _____ and the preferred stock dividend is said to be in _____. Most preferred stock issued in the United States is _____ preferred stock.

6. The market _____ price or _____ value is the market value of the _____ stock the investor would have if the _____ stock is exchanged with the _____ stock. The market conversion _____ is the conversion _____ multiplied by the market _____ of a share of _____ stock. If the market value of the convertible _____ stock exceeds the conversion value, we refer to this difference as the conversion _____.

7. _____ preferred stock gives the issuer the right to _____ it from the _____ at a predetermined price. If the issuing corporation wants to buy back the stock by using the call, they pay the specified call _____. The call _____ may be a(n) _____ amount forever, or may _____ according to a preset _____. The call price is generally _____ than or equal to the _____ or par value of the stock.

8. Because there is no legal _____ to pay the preferred dividend and because _____ and other _____ take precedence if the firm is liquidated, a corporation can provide this _____ in the form of a(n) _____ fund provision. Funds are deposited with a(n) _____ who uses these _____ to periodically _____ preferred stock, buying it from shareholders at a specified price, the _____ fund call price. The trustee retires _____ stock periodically and the firm is better able to meet the _____ payments on the remaining preferred shares.

9. A corporation may combine any of the previously described _____ into its preferred stock _____. If they hope to sell their preferred shares, they must package them in a way that is _____ to investors and at a reasonable _____. Features that give the _____ flexibility, such as a(n) _____ feature, and features that give the

_____ something of additional value, such as a(n) _____ feature, must be balanced in order to obtain an optimal cost for the package. Packaging a new issue of preferred stock requires considering investors' need for greater _____ and lower _____ and the issuer's need for greater _____ and lower _____.

SHORT ANSWER QUESTIONS

Refer to Chapter 17, pages 571–580 in _Financial Management and Analysis_.

1. What is participating preferred stock and why are there few of these issues?

2. Explain the differences between convertible preferred stock and mandatory convertible preferred stock. Which are preferred by investors and which by issuers?

3. Are there voting rights attached to preferred stock?

4. What factors influence an investor's decision to convert callable preferred stock?

5. What are the advantages and disadvantages for a company issuing preferred stock?

PROBLEMS

Refer to Chapter 17, pages 571–580 in *Financial Management and Analysis*.

1. Semi-Nowl Corporation has 1.1 million shares of 8% cumulative preferred stock outstanding with a stated value of $100 per share. If dividends are not paid for four years, what will be the amount of arrearage?

2. Suppose you own 500 shares of FSU Inc. 12% convertible preferred stock. If each preferred share is convertible into 25 common shares, what is the conversion value of your 5,000 preferred shares if the common stock is trading at $30 per share?

3. KLM Company issued $3 million of 9.75% $80 par preferred shares in 2001. Calculate the total amount of dividends paid on this issue per year and the annual amount of the dividends per share.

CHAPTER 18

Capital Structure

FILL IN THE BLANKS

Refer to Chapter 18, pages 583–621 in *Financial Management and Analysis.*

1. The combination of _____ and equity used to _____ a firm's projects is referred to as its _____ structure. The _____ structure of a firm is some mix of debt, internally generated _____, and new _____.

2. Failure to pay _____ or principal as promised may result in _____ distress. _____ distress is the condition where a firm makes _____ under pressure to satisfy its legal obligations to its _____. These decisions may _____ be in the best interest of the owners of the firm.

3. When _____ financing is used instead of _____, the owners don't share the earnings, all they must do is pay their _____ the interest on

debt. But when _____ financing is used instead of _____, the owners must _____ the increased earnings with the additional owners, diluting their _____ on equity and _____ per share.

4. We can measure the _____ associated with alternative forms of financing by calculating the _____ deviation and the _____ of variation of the possible earnings per share. The _____ the _____ deviation and _____ of variation the _____ the risk.

5. The discount _____ is referred to as the _____ rate, which is the _____ rate that translates _____ earnings into a current _____. The _____ rate reflects the uncertainty associated with the expected earnings in the _____. The more _____ the future earnings, the _____ a dollar of future income is worth today and the _____ the capitalization rate.

6. The risk _____ is the difference between the _____ rate for the net _____ to owners and the _____ rate on _____ to creditors (the _____), which is assumed to be risk _____. The _____ the use of _____, the _____ the _____ premium.

7. The benefit from interest deductibility is referred to as the interest _____. It is equal to the _____ tax rate times the interest _____. An alternative calculation is the _____ tax rate times the _____ rate on debt times the face _____ of debt.

8. If a firm has deductions that _____ income, the result is a net _____ loss. The firm does not have to pay _____ in the year of the _____ and may carry this _____ to another tax year. This _____ may be applied against _____ years' taxable _____, with some limits.

9. For firms whose owners have _____ liability, the more the _____ are financed with _____, the greater the incentive to take on _____ projects, leaving _____ "holding the bag" if the projects turn out to be _____. There is a(n) _____ of interest between _____ interests and _____ interests.

10. We can classify _____ costs into _____ and _____ costs. _____ costs include the legal, administrative, and _____ costs associated with the filing for bankruptcy and the administration of bankruptcy. The _____ costs of bankruptcy are more _____ to evaluate.

SHORT ANSWER QUESTIONS

Refer to Chapter 18, pages 583–621 in *Financial Management and Analysis.*

1. Why can debt financing be more attractive than equity financing?

2. Why do debt ratios differ across industries? Within industries?

3. What is the leverage effect? What happens if earnings are insufficient to cover interest payments?

4. How does the tax shield affect the value of the firm?

5. What is the relationship between financial distress and capital structure? What are the factors to be considered?

6. What factors should be taken into consideration in capital structure decisions?

PROBLEMS

Refer to Chapter 18, pages 583–621 in *Financial Management and Analysis*.

1. Firm Z has $34,000 in debt and $50,000 in equity. What is Firm Z's debt ratio and debt-to-assets ratio? What do the ratios mean?

2. What is the capitalization rate for equity for Firm Z in problem 1, assuming there are no taxes and the cost of equity is 9% and the cost of debt is 5%?

3. Finance-R-Us is considering three possible financing arrangements to raise $1 million of new capital. Currently, the capital structure consists of no debt and $250,000 in equity. There are 100,000 shares of common stock currently outstanding, selling at $2.50 per share. Expected earnings of $200,000, before interest and taxes, are expected for next period. The interest rate on any debt obtained should be 10%. Calculate the earnings to owners, earnings per share, and the distribution of income between creditors, shareholders, and the government for the following three alternatives:

■ Alternative 1: Finance with only new equity.

■ Alternative 2: Finance using 50% debt and 50% equity.

■ Alternative 3: Finance using only new debt.

4. The O.K. Company has $100,000 of debt in its capital structure. The interest rate on this debt is 12%. What is the present value of the tax shield from interest deductibility if the corporate tax rate on income is 35%?

CHAPTER 19

Management of Cash and Marketable Securities

FILL IN THE BLANKS

Refer to Chapter 19, pages 627–648 in *Financial Management and Analysis*.

1. The _____ cycle in part determines how long it takes for a firm to _____ cash from its short-term _____ and, therefore, the _____ and cost of its investment in _____ assets, or _____ capital. Working capital is the capital that managers can immediately put to work to generate the _____ of capital investment. Working capital is also known as _____ capital or _____ capital.

2. The firm's _____ cycle is the time it takes the firm to turn its investment in inventory into cash. It affects how much the firm ties up in _____ assets. The operating cycle comprises the time it takes to: _____ the goods, _____ them, and _____ on their sale. The _____ operating cycle considers the

benefit from purchasing goods on _____ and is the operating cycle less the number of days of on which the account is still owed. The _____ the net operating cycle, the _____ the investment in current assets.

3. Cash flows _____ of a firm as it pays for the goods and services it _____ from others. Cash flows _____ the firm as customers _____ for the goods and services they _____. When we refer to cash, we mean the amount of _____ and _____ assets—currency, coin, and bank balances. When we refer to cash _____, we mean management of cash _____ and _____, as well as the stock of _____ on hand.

4. There is always some degree of _____ about future cash needs. Firms typically hold an additional balance, referred to as a(n) _____ balance, just in case transactions _____ exceed the transactions _____. But how much to keep as a(n) _____ depends on the _____ of the transactions uncertainty—how well we can _____ our transactions needs.

5. If a firm needs cash, it must either _____ an asset or _____ cash. There are _____ costs associated with either. _____ costs are the fees, _____, or other costs associated with _____ assets or _____ to get cash;

they are analogous to the ordering costs for _____.

6. Speeding up _____ cash is done by using a(n) _____ system, through the selection of _____, processing the _____ within the firm, _____ collection, and _____ banking. A(n) _____ is a location where banks meet to exchange checks drawn on each other, and a clearinghouse bank is a participant in a clearinghouse. Being a member of a clearinghouse can _____ check clearing time by up to one-half a day relative to clearing checks through the _____ system. A(n) _____ bank is a bank that has an agreement with a clearinghouse bank to exchange its checks in the clearinghouse.

7. In addition to speeding up incoming cash, _____ down payment of cash is important. It can be done through _____ disbursements by _____ bank balances by depositing only what is needed to make _____ demands on the account and _____ disbursement by paying what is _____ with checks drawn on a bank that is _____ readily accessible to the payee, _____ the check processing _____.

8. The primary role of marketable securities is to store cash that isn't needed _____, but may be needed soon. Examples of these securities are _____ of

deposit, _____ paper, _____ deposits, and _____ bills. When evaluating the _____ of the investment, the following _____ should be considered: _____ risk, _____ power risk, _____ rate risk, _____ rate risk, and _____ risk.

SHORT ANSWER QUESTIONS

Refer to Chapter 19, pages 627–648 in *Financial Management and Analysis*.

1. What factors determine a firm's investment in current assets? What types of firms have more investment in current assets than others?

2. What is cash forecasting and what is its relationship to the operating cycle and net operating cycle?

3. Why would a firm hold cash balances?

4. How much cash should a firm hold and what are the costs associated with doing so?

5. What is the lockbox system and how does it function?

PROBLEMS

Refer to Chapter 19, pages 627–648 in *Financial Management and Analysis*.

1. P&R Corporation uses about $1 million in cash each month. The sale of marketable securities to meet any cash deficiencies costs the firm $100 per transaction. P&R

invests its short-term funds in securities which earn an average of 7%.

a. If each time the firm needs cash it sells $400,000 of securities, what is the holding cost associated with the cash investment?

b. If each time the firm needs cash it sells $400,000 of securities, what are the transaction costs associated with the cash investment?

c. Using the Baumol model, what level of cash infusion minimizes costs associated with cash?

2. Assume that the cash flows vary throughout the year. Because of uncertainty surrounding the cash flows, P&R has decided to carry a minimum balance of $500,000 in cash. The variance of the daily cash flows is $75,000. They operate on a 365-day year.

a. At what point will a new cash infusion be needed?

b. At what point should excess cash be invested in marketable securities?

3. DOWNS Shipping ships packages nationwide. Its collection float averages $250,000 a day. DOWNS is considering a lockbox system which was proposed by its bank in Omaha, Nebraska, because it is in the middle of the country. The system will cost the firm $35,000, but it is estimated that it will reduce the collection float by three days. Additional processing costs of $5,000 a year will be saved by the firm because the payments will be sent directly to the bank. The system will necessitate the use of wire transfers, which will cost the firm $9,000 per year. If DOWNS can earn 10% on its short-term investments, is the system worthwhile?

4. Jewlez, Inc. is a precious stone importer and wholesaler. Jewelz sells approximately 400,000 cut and polished stones each year. The sales occur uniformly throughout the year. Because of high insurance fees, the carrying cost is $7 per stone. Due to the fact that most of its orders from customers are in advance, Jewelz can let its inventory drop to zero before reordering. It costs the firm $190 each time it orders and Jewelz currently orders 5,000 stones at a time. Is this the most cost effective order size?

CHAPTER 20

Management of Receivables and Inventory

FILL IN THE BLANKS

Refer to Chapter 20, pages 651–673 in *Financial Management And Analysis*.

1. The majority of a firm's investment is in _____ assets, however, it is tied up in accounts _____ and _____ which represent investments that are necessary for day-to-day _____ of the business. A firm needs _____ so that it will have _____ to sell and the _____ of inventory differs among firms largely because of the _____ of the products they sell.

2. Firms extend _____ to customers to help stimulate _____. Extending _____ is both a(n) _____ and a(n) _____ decision. When a firm extends credit to its customers, it does so to encourage _____ of its goods and _____.

The most direct _____ is the _____ on the increased sales.

3. The _____ cost is similar to the _____ cost that we looked at for cash balances: the product of the _____ cost of investing in accounts receivable and the _____ in the accounts. The _____ cost is the _____ the firm could have earned on its next best _____. The investment is the amount the firm has _____ to generate _____.

4. The effective cost of trade _____ for a customer is calculated by determining the effective _____ cost for the length of time the credit is extended. _____ this cost makes it _____ with the cost of other forms of credit.

5. _____ terms consist of the _____ amount of credit, the length of period allowed for _____, and the _____ rate and _____ period, if any. The purpose of _____ is to attract _____, thereby increasing _____, and to encourage the early _____ of accounts, thereby reducing the amount tied up in accounts _____.

6. _____ policies specify the procedures for collecting _____ accounts. Collection could start with

polite _____, continuing in progressively _____ steps, and ending by placing the account in the hands of a(n) _____ agency. In designing the collection procedures, you must keep in mind that _____ efforts to collect may result in _____ future sales.

7. _____ how well accounts _____ are managed can be done using financial _____ and _____ schedules. Financial _____ can be used to get an overall picture of how fast collection is going on accounts _____. _____ schedules, which are breakdowns of accounts receivable by how _____ they have been around, help give a more detailed picture of the _____ efforts.

8. Ideally, a firm wants to design its _____ policy so that the marginal _____ from extending _____ equals its marginal _____ of extending credit. At this point, the firm _____ owners' wealth. But the benefits and costs are _____. The best the firm can do in _____ the benefits and costs from its credit and collection policies is to learn from its own _____ or from the experience of others.

9. Some firms choose to form a wholly-owned _____, that is, a corporation _____ by the parent firm in order to provide the _____ granting and _____ function of the parent firm. The sole

purpose of _____ finance subsidiaries is to _____ the customers' purchase of the parent firm's _____. These subsidiaries can stimulate _____ by providing easy access to _____.

10. _____ is the stock of physical goods for eventual sale. _____ consists of raw material, work-in-process, and finished goods available for _____. There are many _____ in a decision of how much inventory to have on hand. As with accounts receivable, there is a trade-off between the costs of _____ in inventory and the costs of _____ inventory. There's a cost to too much _____ and there's a cost of too _____ inventory.

11. _____ inventory can be done by looking at financial _____ in much the same way we can monitor receivables. The number of days of _____ is the ratio of the dollar value of _____ at a point in time to the cost of goods sold per day. This ratio is an estimate of the number of _____ worth of _____ you have on hand. Combined with an estimate of the _____ for your goods, this ratio helps you in planning your _____ and _____ of goods. The inventory turnover ratio tells, on average, how many times _____ flows through the firm—from raw materials to goods sold—during the period.

SHORT ANSWER QUESTIONS

Refer to Chapter 20, pages 651–673 in *Financial Management and Analysis.*

1. What is the relationship between a firm extending credit and accounts receivable?

2. What are the implicit costs with granting discounts? What are the costs of credit?

3. What factors should be considered when extending credit?

4. What factors influence the assessment of credit?

5. What are the reasons for holding inventory?

6. Explain the two models of inventory management.

PROBLEMS

Refer to Chapter 20, pages 651–673 in *Financial Management and Analysis*.

1. The Retton Corporation currently offers terms of 2/20, net 60 to its customers and is considering a change to 4/15, net 60. The credit manager believes that this will reduce the firm's days of credit from the current 40 days to 30

days, in addition to increasing sales due to the higher discount. Sales are expected to increase from the present $500,000 to $800,000. About 60% of Retton's customers take the discount now, and it is estimated that the percentage will increase to 75%. The firm plans to maintain its present contribution margin of 30%. Processing costs and bad debt losses are not expected to change. Retton can earn 12% on its short-term investments.

a. What is the current cost of trade credit for Retton's customers, and what will it be if Retton makes the proposed change?

b. What is the cost to Retton for changing the discount?

c. What is the change in the carrying cost of accounts receivable for Retton?

d. Should Retton make the change?

CHAPTER 21

Management of Short-Term Financing

FILL IN THE BLANKS

Refer to Chapter 21, pages 679–714 in *Financial Management and Analysis*.

1. A corporation invests in short-term assets, such as _____, accounts _____, inventory, and marketable _____. Short-term assets are also referred to as _____ capital, because they are put to work to generate sales, which eventually result in cash flow that ultimately generates _____. _____ capital comprises _____ working capital, the investment necessary to satisfy the _____ demands of _____, and _____ working capital, the _____ between actual working capital and permanent working capital.

2. The _____ cost of borrowing is the cost of _____, considering both _____ and _____ costs. This effective cost is the cost of

_____ for a given period, the duration of time over which interest is paid and at the end of which _____ is calculated.

3. _____ credit is granted by a supplier to a customer purchasing _____ or _____. _____ credit arises as the customer acquires goods or services and promises to pay in the _____. From the _____ point of view, trade credit is a way of making more _____. From the _____ point of view, trade credit is an easy way to finance the _____ of goods. For the _____, trade credit creates accounts _____; for the _____, trade credit creates accounts _____.

4. Managing accounts _____ involves negotiating the terms of _____, as well as deciding when to pay amounts due. Remember that accounts _____ are the "flip side" of accounts _____—accounts payable are someone else's accounts receivable. Suppliers are trying to _____ costs, in terms of funds tied up in accounts receivables and bad debts. Yet, at the same time, they are extending _____ to generate more _____.

5. Firms try to set policies so terms of credit are _____ within industries. However, if a firm is an important _____ of a particular supplier, _____ terms of credit may be negotiated. In cal-

culating the _____ of trade credit, managers know that paying within the _____ period uses free credit—meaning that payment can be _____ and then paid the same as cash on the date of purchase. Also, paying _____ the discount period _____ the cost of credit.

6. _____ financing is backed by some specific _____ or assets of the borrower. A borrower's _____ used in this way are referred to as _____. The _____ acts as a backup source of _____ for the lender if the borrower fails to abide by the terms of the loan. The collateral for short-term financing arrangements are usually _____ assets—_____ securities, accounts _____, or _____.

7. Accounts _____ can be used as collateral for a(n) _____ loan. There are three types of financing arrangements that use accounts _____ as security: _____, _____, and _____. Securitizing assets, also referred to as asset _____, is an important financing arrangement for raising _____ to _____ term funds.

8. In an assignment of _____, the lender makes a loan accepting the borrower's accounts _____ as the _____. The borrower receives immediate _____ in exchange for a(n) _____

note to the lender. The borrower's customers are generally instructed to send their payments to the lender, who uses these payments to reduce the _____ of the loan.

9. Instead of simply using accounts _____ as _____, the borrower can _____ them outright to another party—called a(n) _____— typically a bank or a commercial finance company. Selling the _____—called factoring—may be done with or without recourse. The factor performs all the accounts receivable functions: evaluating customers' _____, approving _____, and _____ on accounts receivable.

10. A(n) _____ agreement, also referred to as a(n) _____, is the sale of a security with a commitment by the seller to buy the same security back from the purchaser at a specified price at a designated future date. The seller repurchases the security at the repurchase _____, on the repurchase _____. A repurchase agreement is a(n) _____ loan, where the collateral is the _____. The interest rate is the _____ rate. When the term of the loan is one day, it is a(n) _____ repo and a loan for more than one day is called a(n) _____ repo.

SHORT ANSWER QUESTIONS

Refer to Chapter 21, pages 679–714 in *Financial Management and Analysis*.

1. What are the costs of borrowing for all manner of loans?

2. What is the difference between secured and unsecured financing?

3. Why is it that as the credit period lengthens, the cost of trade credit declines?

4. When managing accounts payable, what are the consequences of paying late?

5. Why might high and low turnover be good?

6. What are the types of financing arrangements and some of their characteristics?

PROBLEMS

Refer to Chapter 21, pages 679–714 in *Financial Management and Analysis*.

1. The CZ company is trying to decide among four different financing alternatives to finance $100,000:

a. Bank A has offered to lend the firm the whole amount for six months at an APR of 16%. The bank will require a compensating balance of 17% of the face value of the loan and will charge a $1,000 loan origination fee.

b. Bank B has offered to lend the entire amount for three months at an APR of 20%. The loan is a discount loan, and Bank B requires a compensating balance requirement of 10%.

c. Bank C has offered to lend the firm the entire amount for one month at an APR of 24%. The loan is a single-payment loan with interest and principal to be paid at the end of the month. There is no compensating balance requirement and no loan origination fee.

d. CZ can forgo its supplier discounts for the month. The credit terms are 3/10, net 45.

Which is the cheapest source of financing?

2. The Safe-T Corporation used a repurchase agreement to meet its need for short-term financing. It received $9.5 million for the sale of $10 million in face value of U.S. Treasury bills that had a market value of $9.7 million, and

it repurchased the bills thirty days later for $9.6 million. What is the effective annual cost?

3. Rustee Iron Works is considering using a field warehouse loan as part of its short-term financing. It will require a loan of $1 million. Interest on the loan will be at an annual rate of 11%, single-payment interest, paid at the end of the year. The field warehouse charges 3.5% of the face value of the loan, payable at the beginning of the year. What is the effective cost of the warehousing arrangement?

4. Can-Do Corporation has issued five-month commercial paper with a $250,000 face value. The firm's proceeds

from the sale of the paper are $237,500. What is the effective annual cost of this loan?

5. The Bags-O-Chips Company wants to use $800,000 of accounts receivable to secure financing for the next month. We're #1 Finance Company is willing to lend Chips 65% of the face value of the receivables at 40 basis points above the prime rate, which is currently 4% APR. We're #2 Finance Company will factor Chips receivables, advancing 80% of the receivables and charging a fee of 2% of Chips total receivables. This fee will be paid up front. Interest will be at 30 basis points above the prime rate. We're #2 also will be performing all credit functions, saving Chips an estimated $4,000 for the month. Which arrangement is least costly?

CHAPTER 22

Financial Ratio Analysis

FILL IN THE BLANKS

Refer to Chapter 22, pages 721–765 in *Financial Management and Analysis*.

1. A(n) _____ is a mathematical relation between two quantities. A financial _____ is a(n) _____ between one bit of financial information and another. Ratios can be classified according to the way they are _____ and the financial _____ they are describing. There are as many different financial ratios as there are possible _____ of items appearing on financial _____.

2. Return-on-_____ ratios compare measures of _____, such as earnings or net income, with measures of _____. The return on _____, also called the basic earning _____ ratio, is the ratio of _____ earnings to total assets. The return on _____ is the ratio of the net _____ shareholders receive to their _____ in the stock.

3. The method of analyzing _____ ratios in terms of _____ margin and _____ ratios, referred to as the _____ System, is credited to the E.I. Du Pont Corporation. Du Pont's management developed this system of breaking down return ratios into their _____ to help managers understand the "_____" behind the firm's _____.

4. _____ reflects the ability of a firm to meet its _____-term obligations using those assets that are most readily converted into _____. Assets that may be converted into _____ in a short period of time are referred to as _____ assets; they are listed in financial statements as _____ assets. _____ assets are often referred to as _____ capital, because they represent the resources needed for the _____ operations of the firm's long-term capital investments.

5. How much liquidity a firm needs depends on its _____ cycle. The _____ cycle is the duration from the time _____ is invested in goods and _____ to the time that investment produces _____. The _____ the _____ cycle, the _____ the amount of net _____ capital required.

6. _____ margin ratios compare components of _____ with _____. They give us an

idea of what factors make up a firm's _____ and are usually expressed as a portion of each _____ of sales. The analyst would focus on _____ profit (sales less cost of goods sold), a measure of income that is the direct result of _____ management. Comparing _____ profit with _____ produces the gross profit margin.

7. _____ ratios, or turnover ratios, can be used to evaluate the benefits produced by specific _____, such as _____ or accounts _____ or to evaluate the benefits produced by the totality of the firm's assets. The _____ turnover ratio indicates how quickly a firm has used inventory to generate the _____ and _____ sold. The accounts _____ turnover ratio measures how effectively a firm uses _____ extended to customers. The _____ turnover ratio tells how many times during the year the _____ of a firm's total assets is generated in _____.

8. Financial _____ is associated with a firm's ability to satisfy its _____ obligations, and is often measured using the extent to which _____ financing is used relative to _____. Financial _____ ratios are used to assess how much financial _____ the firm has taken on. There are two types of financial _____ ratios: _____ percentages and _____ ratios.

9. _____ coverage ratio, also called times _____ ratio, measures a firm's ability to handle financial _____. This ratio indicates how well the firm can meet the _____ payments associated with _____. The _____ the interest coverage ratio, the _____ able the firm is to pay its _____ expenses.

10. _____ analysis is a method of analysis in which the components of a financial _____ are compared with each other. The first step in _____ analysis is to break down a financial statement—either the _____ sheet or the _____ statement—into its parts. The next step is to _____ the proportion that each item represents relative to some _____. In common-size analysis of the _____ sheet, the benchmark is total _____. For the _____ statement, the benchmark is _____.

SHORT ANSWER QUESTIONS

Refer to Chapter 22, pages 721–765 in *Financial Management and Analysis.*

1. How is financial information presented? How is the information classified?

2. What aspects of operating performance and financial condition do financial ratios evaluate?

3. What is the Du Pont System and how is it used?

4. What is the difference between book value and market value and how does it affect financial ratio analysis?

5. Are there any concerns and/or cautions when using financial ratios?

PROBLEMS

Refer to Chapter 22, pages 721–765 in *Financial Management and Analysis*.

1. Using Wang Laboratories' balance sheet and income statement for the year ending June 30, 1995, shown on page 773 of *Financial Management and Analysis*, make the following calculations assuming a 365-day year, all sales and purchases are on credit, and that the financial data is in hundreds of thousands:

a. Current ratio

b. Quick ratio

c. Inventory turnover ratio

d. Total asset turnover ratio

e. Gross profit margin

f. Operating profit margin

g. Net profit margin

h. Debt-to-assets ratio

i. Debt-to-equity ratio

j. Return on assets (basic earning power)

k. Return on equity

l. Number of days of inventory

m. Number of days of credit

n. Number of days of purchases

o. Operating cycle

p. Net operating cycle

2. Use the information from problem 1 to answer the following: Given the following industry average ratios, what is Wang's standing as it emerges from bankruptcy?

Current ratio	2 times
Quick ratio	1 times
Number of days of credit	90 days
Inventory turnover	35 times
Total asset turnover	3 times
Debt-to-equity ratio	45%
Operating profit margin	10%
Net profit margin	7%
Return on assets	9%
Return on equity	11%

CHAPTER 23

Earnings Analysis

FILL IN THE BLANKS

Refer to Chapter 23, pages 775–796 in *Financial Management and Analysis*.

1. The theory of stock _____ makes sense. If a company's _____ cash flows could accurately be _____, then the value of the company's _____ today could be determined. Therefore the _____ could be classified as _____- or _____-valued by the market.

2. _____ future cash flows is difficult. As an alternative, examination of the _____ and _____ relation between stock prices and some fundamental value information, such as _____ or _____ is needed. Then, using this relation, the _____ of a share of stock can be estimated.

3. Earnings can really mean many different things depending on the context. If a financial analyst is evaluating the per-

formance of a company's _____, the focus is on
_____ earnings or earnings before interest and
taxes, (_____). If the analyst is evaluating the
performance of a company _____, the focus is
on _____, which is EBIT _____ inter-
est and taxes. If the analyst is evaluating the performance
of the company from a(n) _____ perspective, the
earnings are the earnings available to common shareholders—EBIT less interest, taxes, and _____ stock
dividends.

4. We often refer to earnings in terms of the _____
per share of stock, rather than as a total _____
amount generated in a period. Expressing a company's net
_____ in terms of income per _____
allows us to compare it with the company's _____
price per share. Earnings per share (_____) is
earnings available for _____ shareholders, divided
by the number of common shares _____.

5. _____ earnings per share are earnings minus
preferred dividends, divided by the average number of
shares outstanding. _____ earnings per share
are earnings minus preferred dividends, divided by the
number of shares outstanding considering all
_____ securities. Companies that report
_____ per share for any prior period must
_____ these amounts in terms of the new basic
and diluted calculations.

6. The most common financial ratio forecast is _____ earnings per share of a firm, though projections of _____ flows and stock _____ are available. For most companies whose stock is _____-traded, there are a number of _____ who analyze the stock and make forecasts regarding earnings in the future. In addition, several service _____ collect and report statistics of analysts' _____.

7. The _____ earnings forecast is the _____ of the earnings per share for a given stock. Services that provide analyst forecast information also provide earnings _____ analysis, the difference between _____ earnings per share and the _____ earnings per share, where the consensus forecast is used as the _____ earnings per share.

8. _____ earnings forecasts and the forecasts of _____ analysts are used to compute several measures that researchers have found to be important factors in _____ stock returns such as earnings _____, or earnings _____. This is a measure of consensus earnings _____ found by computing the growth in earnings based on actual earnings for the _____ period and the consensus earnings forecasts for the _____ period.

9. Relationships in which EPS in a(n) _____ period is assumed to depend on EPS in one or more _____ periods are called _____ models. Often the data used in forecasting EPS are _____ and _____ EPS of the company, but it is critical that EPS be _____ to reflect changes in accounting requirements. For example, an analyst who used a(n) _____ model would want to adjust _____ reported EPS based on primary, diluted, or fully diluted EPS for the new reporting requirements.

10. Many investors are interested in how the _____ are valued by the market. A measure of how these earnings are valued is the _____ ratio (_____). This ratio compares the _____ per common share with _____ per common share. The result is a multiple—the value of a share of _____ expressed as a multiple of _____ per share. The _____ of this measure is referred to as the earnings _____ (_____).

SHORT ANSWER QUESTIONS

Refer to Chapter 23, pages 775–796 in *Financial Management and Analysis*

1. What determines the market price of common stock?

2. What is earnings management and why is it such a concern?

3. What is the relationship between earnings and stock price?

4. Why do the number of common shares outstanding change? How does the change affect EPS?

5. How accurate are EPS forecasts?

PROBLEMS

Refer to Chapter 23, pages 775–796 in *Financial Management and Analysis*

1. Too-Tired Company had 1.5 million shares of stock outstanding at the beginning of the year and 1.87 million shares at the end of the year. After issuing 0.37 million shares at the beginning of the second quarter, if Too-Tired had earnings available to common shareholders of $6.5 million, what is the company's earnings per share?

2. HiGro Corporation had $1.80 in earnings per share and paid dividends of $0.30 per share in 2001. HiGro was selling for $28.50 a share at the end of 2001. The book value of HiGro's common equity at the time was $22.00 per share. HiGro has no preferred stock.

a. What was HiGro's dividend payout ratio for 2001?

b. What was the P/E ratio at the end of 2001?

c. Are investors willing to pay more for the stock than its earnings per share?

3. For the 1999 fiscal year, Outtel Corporation had net income of $4,355 million. At the beginning of the year, there were 1,323 million shares outstanding and at the end of the year there were 1,300 million shares. There are 300 million potentially dilutive shares during 1999 from employee stock option plans and warrants. Calculate the basic and diluted earnings per share.

4. The Sagging Bay Company announced earnings of $1.82 per share for the 2002 fiscal year. The consensus analyst forecast for 2002 earnings was $1.95.

    a. Calculate the forecast error for Sagging Bay.

    b. Explain the expected stock price reaction in response to the worse-than-expected earnings.

CHAPTER 24

Cash Flow Analysis

FILL IN THE BLANKS

Refer to Chapter 24, pages 797–817 in *Financial Management and Analysis.*

1. _____ flows are essential ingredients in _____: The value of a company today is the present _____ of its expected _____ cash flows. Therefore, understanding _____ and _____ cash flows may help the analyst in forecasting future cash flows and, hence determine the value of the company, and also may aid in assessing the ability of a firm to maintain current _____ and its current capital _____ policy without relying on external _____.

2. The primary difficulty with _____ a cash flow is that it is a flow: cash flows _____ and cash flows _____ of the company. At any point in time there is a stock of _____ on hand, but it varies among companies because of the _____ of the

company, the cash _____ of the business, and the company's management of _____ capital.

3. From the basic cash flow, the _____ cash needs are subtracted resulting in a cash flow referred to as _____ cash flow. By restructuring the _____ of cash flows in this way, the analyst can see how much _____ the company has when it must make business _____ that may adversely impact the long-term financial _____ of the enterprise.

4. There is _____ one correct method of _____ free cash flow and different analysts may arrive at different estimates for a company. The problem is that because it is impossible to _____ free cash flow as dictated by the theory, so many _____ have arisen to _____ this cash flow.

5. The _____ cash flow (_____) is free cash flow less interest and other financing costs and taxes. In this approach, free cash flow is defined as _____ before depreciation, interest, and taxes _____ capital expenditures. Capital _____ encompass all capital spending, whether for _____ or _____ and no changes in _____ capital are considered.

6. _____ cash flow gives the analyst an idea of the _____ cash flow of the company. This cash flow measure may be useful from a(n) _____ perspective in terms of evaluating the company's _____ to fund additional _____. From a(n) _____ perspective, net cash flow net of dividends may be an appropriate measure because this represents the cash flow that is _____ in the company.

7. A useful ratio to help further assess a company's cash flow is the cash flow to _____ ratio, or _____ coverage ratio. This ratio gives the analyst information about the financial _____ of the company and is particularly useful for _____ -intensive firms and utilities. The _____ the ratio, the _____ the financial flexibility.

8. Another useful cash flow ratio is the cash flow to _____ ratio where debt can be represented as total _____, long-term _____, or a debt measure that captures a specific range of maturity (e.g., debt maturing in 5 years). This ratio gives a measure of a company's _____ to meet maturing _____ obligations, thus it is a measure of a company's _____ quality.

9. The analysis of cash flows provides _____ that can be used along with other financial data to help the

analyst assess the financial _____ of a company. _____ companies tend to have relatively stable relations among the cash flows while _____ companies exhibit declining cash flows from _____ and financing and _____ cash flows for investment one and two years prior to the bankruptcy. Further, _____ companies tend to expend _____ cash flows to financing sources than they bring in during the year prior to bankruptcy.

SHORT ANSWER QUESTIONS

Refer to Chapter 24, pages 797–817 in *Financial Management and Analysis*.

1. What is cash flow and how is it measured?

2. Explain the direct and indirect method of reporting cash flow.

3. What are the patterns of the cash flows for the different types and maturities of firms?

4. What is free cash flow and why is its important?

5. What can cash flow analysis reveal?

PROBLEMS

Refer to Chapter 24, pages 797–817 in *Financial Management and Analysis*.

1. Calculate free cash flow, net free cash flow, and net cash flow for the Krunchy Krust Donuts Company. Their financials are as follows:

Krunchy Krust Donuts, Income Statement, in millions

Total Revenue	**$56**
Cost of revenue	$3
Gross profit	$53
Operating Expenses	
Selling general and administrative expenses	$8
Nonrecurring	($1)
Other operating expenses	$2
Operating income	$24
Total other income and expenses net	($1)
Earnings before interest and taxes	$21
Interest expense	$2
Income before taxes	$19
Income tax expense	$7
Net Income	$12

Krunchy Krust Donuts, Statement of Cash Flows, in millions

Net Income	**$12**
Cash Flow Operating Activities	
Depreciation	$4
Adjustments to net income	$13
Changes in Operating Activities	
Changes in accounts receivables	($3)
Changes in liabilities	($10)
Changes in inventories	($2)
Changes in other operating activities	($2)
Cash flows from operating activities	$12
Cash Flow Investing Activities	
Capital expenditures	($15)
Investments	$7
Other cash flows from investing activities	($31)
Cash flows from investing activities	($39)
Cash Flow Financing Activities	
Sale/Purchase of stock	$8
Net borrowings	$3
Other cash flows from financing activities	($2)
Cash dividends paid	($2)
Cash flows from financing activities	$7
Change in cash and cash equivalents	**($20)**

CHAPTER 25

International Financial Management

FILL IN THE BLANKS

Refer to Chapter 25, pages 823–858 in *Financial Management and Analysis.*

1. Financial management decisions of most firms are not confined to _____ borders. Many _____ and _____ decisions involve economies and firms outside a firm's own domestic borders either directly, through _____ transactions, or indirectly, through the effects of international issues on the _____ economy. International _____ management is the management of a firm's assets and liabilities considering the _____ economy in which the firm operates.

2. Trends and agreements throughout the twentieth century reduced _____. The General _____ on _____ and Trade (GATT) is a forum for negotiating the reduction in trade _____ on a multilat-

eral basis. Monetary cooperation and international trade is facilitated through the _____ Fund (_____). The _____ Union (E.U.) is an organization whose goal is to increase _____ cooperation and integration among its European member countries. The North _____ Free _____ Agreement (_____) is a pact among Canada, Mexico, and the United States for the gradual removal of trade barriers for most _____ produced and sold in North America.

3. A(n) _____ company is a firm that does business in two or more _____. Most large U.S. corporations are _____ firms, deriving a large part of their income from operations beyond the U.S. _____. Companies expand beyond their _____ borders for many reasons, including: To gain access to new _____, to achieve _____ efficiency, to gain access to _____, to reduce political and regulatory _____, to diversify, and to gain access to _____.

4. Financial managers must be aware of the issues relating to multiple _____. In particular, the financial manager must be aware of _____ rates and the related _____ risk. The _____ rate is the number of units of a given currency that can be purchased for one unit of another country's _____; the exchange rate tells us about the relative _____ of any two currencies. Currency risk or _____ risk is

the risk that the relative values of the domestic and foreign currencies will _____ change.

5. When a currency _____ value relative to other currencies, we say that the currency has _____ if the change is due to changes in supply and demand, or been _____ if the change is due to government intervention. If the currency _____ value relative other currencies, we say that the currency has _____ or been _____.

6. If there are _____ barriers or costs to trade across borders, the _____ of a given product will be the _____ regardless of where it is sold. This is referred to as the law of _____ price: Where there are different _____ on either side of the border, after adjusting for the difference in currencies, the _____ of a good or service is the same across borders. In the case of different currencies, the law of one price is known as _____ (_____).

7. Taxes paid by corporate entities can be classified into two types: _____ taxes and _____ taxes. The former includes taxes paid to the _____ government based on _____ income and possibly any _____ income taxes. Indirect taxes include real estate appreciation, _____ taxes, and miscellaneous taxes on _____ transactions.

8. It is common for a company's _____ in different countries to buy and sell goods from each other. The price for the goods in such _____ transactions is called a(n) _____ price. Establishing transfer prices to promote goal _____ within a(n) _____ company is a complicated topic. In practice, a primary goal in the establishment of transfer prices is the minimization of worldwide _____, _____ taxes and _____ duty taxes.

9. A corporation is not limited to raising funds in the capital market where it is domiciled. _____ means the _____ of capital markets throughout the world into a global capital market. From the perspective of a given country, capital markets can be classified into two markets: either a(n) _____ market or a(n) _____ market, and a(n) _____ market. It can be decomposed into two parts: the _____ market and the _____ market. The _____ market is where issuers _____ in the country issue securities and where those securities are subsequently _____.

10. The world capital markets can be classified as either completely _____ or completely _____. In a completely _____ capital market, investors in one country are _____ permitted to invest in the securities issued by an entity in another country. In a completely _____ capital market there are _____ restrictions to prevent investors from

investing in securities issued in any capital market throughout the world. Real-world capital markets are _____ completely segmented nor completely integrated, but fall somewhere in between and are _____ segmented or _____ integrated.

11. A corporate treasurer seeking to raise funds via a(n) _____ offering can issue in the _____ sector of another country's bond market or the _____. The distinguishing features of the securities in this market are that they are _____ by an international syndicate, at issuance they are offered _____ to investors in a number of countries, they are issued _____ the jurisdiction of any single country, and they are in _____ form. The sector of the Euromarket in which bonds are traded is called the _____ market.

12. The important elements of cash flows, _____ of capital, and analysis are present in the _____ capital budgeting decision whether the investment is _____ or _____. There are several sources of the added complexity: _____ currency risk, restrictions on _____, and _____ risk. These risks and _____ affect not only an investment's cost of _____ but also make the estimation of cash flows all the more difficult.

SHORT ANSWER QUESTIONS

Refer to Chapter 25, pages 823–858 in *Financial Management and Analysis*.

1. Why would a firm participate in the international market?

2. What is free trade?

3. How are corporations taxed?

4. How is taxable income determined?

5. What are IDRs and ADRs?

PROBLEMS

Refer to Chapter 25, pages 823–858 in *Financial Management and Analysis*.

1. Consider the following exchange rates:

   ■ U.S. $1 to 1,598 Venezuelan Bolivar's
   ■ U.S. $1 to 1.56 Australian dollars

   a. Calculate the exchange rate of Venezuelan Bolivar's to an Australian dollar.

   b. Calculate the exchange rate of Australian dollars to a Venezuelan Bolivar.

3. Suppose that the exchange rate for U.S. $1 for another currency is such that U.S. $1 = 3.5 ARS (Argentine pesos). Further suppose that if the exchange rate remains the same, you will receive a 25% return on your investment in ARS currency over the next year's period. As an investor, you are aware of the volatility in Argentina's currency exchange so sudden movements are expected.

a. If the exchange rate were to change such that $1 = 50 ARS, what return do you expect on the investment?

b. If the exchange rate were to change such that $1 = 2 ARS, what return do you expect on the investment?

3. The 3W company is a U.S. corporation with a subsidiary in another country. 3W's U.S. corporate marginal tax rate is 40% and the subsidiary operating in a foreign country has a marginal tax rate of 52%. 3W manufactures a product for U.S. $10 a unit and sells 2 million units at cost to the subsidiary who further finishes the unit for another $10 per unit and sells the completed product for $190 per unit. The fixed costs for 3W and the subsidiary are $1 million and $0.5 million, respectively.

   a. What are the taxes and the net income of the parent, the subsidiary, and the company as a whole if the transfer price is set at $30 per unit? Include the worldwide net income and taxes.

b. What are the taxes and the net income of the parent, the subsidiary, and the company as a whole if the transfer price is raised to $50 per unit? Include the worldwide net income and taxes.

CHAPTER 26

Borrowing Via Structured Finance Transactions

FILL IN THE BLANKS

Refer to Chapter 26 pages 861–880 in *Financial Management and Analysis.*

1. As an alternative to the issuance of a corporate _____, a corporation can issue a security backed by _____ or _____. Securities that have loans or receivables as their _____ are referred to as _____-backed securities. The transaction in which asset-backed securities are created is referred to as a structured _____ transaction or as a(n) _____ financing.

2. An issuer seeking to raise funds via a(n) _____ financing must establish itself as an issuer in the _____-backed securities market. Once an issuer establishes itself in the market, it can look at both the corporate _____ market and the _____-backed securities market to determine the better

_____ source. It will compare the _____ of funds in the corporate bond market and the asset-backed securities market and select the one with the _____ cost.

3. Analysis of the _____ quality of the collateral depends on the _____ type. The _____ agencies will look at the underlying borrower's _____ to pay and the borrower's _____ in the asset. The borrower is the individual or business entity that took out the _____. The borrower's equity will be a key _____ as to whether a borrower has an economic incentive to _____ or to _____ the asset and pay off a(n) _____.

4. While viewed as a(n) _____-party, in many asset-backed securities transactions, the _____ is effectively the _____ of the loans used as the collateral of the corporation seeking funding. The servicer also may be responsible for advancing _____ when there are _____ in payments that result in a temporary shortfall in payments to the investors in the securities issued in a structured _____ transaction.

5. _____ agencies look at the ability of a(n) _____ to perform all the activities that a(n) _____ will be responsible for before they assign a(n) _____ rating to the bonds issued. If a(n)

_____ is unacceptable, a structured finance transaction will _____ be rated. The rating agency may require a(n) _____ servicer if there is a concern about the ability of a servicer to perform.

6. Ratings companies analyze the _____ of cash flow payments to test whether the collateral's cash _____ match the _____ that must be made to satisfy the issuer's _____. This requires that the rating company make assumptions about _____ and delinquencies under various interest _____ scenarios. Based on its analysis of the collateral and the _____ testing of the structure to assess the _____ that the bondholders will _____ be repaid in full, a rating agency will determine the amount of _____ enhancement necessary for an issue to receive a particular _____ rating.

7. The way credit _____ works is that some third party is either paid a(n) _____ or a(n) _____ premium or earns extra _____ on a security in the structure to assume _____ risk. _____ credit enhancement involves third-party guarantees such as insurance or a letter of _____. _____ credit enhancement includes overcollateralization, _____-subordinated structure, and reserves. Deals will often have _____ than one form of credit enhancement. The rating agencies specify the amount of credit enhancement to obtain a(n) _____ credit rating.

8. Perhaps the _____ form of credit enhancement to understand is _____ or a letter of credit. In this form of credit enhancement, a(n) _____ provider agrees, for a fee, to _____ the performance of a certain amount of the collateral against defaults. Perhaps the biggest perceived disadvantage to this form of credit enhancement is so called _____ risk. If the credit enhancement provider is _____ then the bonds guaranteed by the enhancement provider are typically _____ as well.

9. The _____-subordinate structure is another form of _____ credit enhancement that involves the subordination of some _____ classes for the benefit of attaining a high investment-grade rating for other bond classes. A structure can have _____ bond classes. The _____ that must be offered on the bond classes are affected by the _____ demanded by investors. The _____ the credit rating of the bond class, the _____ yield is demanded and the _____ will be the proceeds received from the sale of the bonds for that class.

10. _____ funds come in two forms: _____ reserve funds and excess _____. _____ reserve funds are straight deposits of cash generated from issuance proceeds. In this case, part of the underwriting profits from the deal are _____ into a fund and used to _____ any losses. Excess _____ accounts involve the allocation of excess spread into a sepa-

rate reserve account after paying out the _____ to bondholders, the servicing _____, and all other _____ on a monthly basis.

SHORT ANSWER QUESTIONS

Refer to Chapter 26 pages 861–880 in *Financial Management and Analysis.*

1. What is a structured finance transaction?

2. Why use a structured finance transaction?

3. What is a captive finance company?

4. What do rating agencies look at in rating asset-backed securities?

CHAPTER 27

Equipment Leasing

FILL IN THE BLANKS

Refer to Chapter 27, pages 883–914 in *Financial Management and Analysis*.

1. A(n) _____ is a contract wherein, over the term of the _____, the owner of the equipment permits another entity to use it in exchange for a promise by the latter to make a series of _____. The owner of the equipment is referred to as the _____. The entity that is being granted permission to use the equipment is referred to as the _____.

2. _____ leases fall into two general categories: _____-oriented leases and _____-oriented true leases. _____-oriented leases, also referred to as _____ leases, transfer all incidents of ownership of the leased property to the lessee and usually give the lessee a fixed _____, bargain purchase option, or _____ option not based on fair market value at the time of exercise. Substantial cost savings

can often be achieved through the use of _____-oriented true leases in which the _____ claims and retains the tax benefits of ownership and passes through to the _____ a portion of such tax benefits in the form of reduced lease payments.

3. The most frequent _____ cited by _____ company representatives and _____ is that leasing _____ working capital. The reasoning is as follows: When a firm _____ money to purchase equipment, the lending institution rarely provides an amount _____ to the entire price of the equipment to be financed. Instead, the lender requires the _____ firm to take a(n) _____ position in the equipment by making a down _____.

4. The amount of the down _____ will depend on such factors as the type of _____, the _____ of the borrower, and prevailing _____ conditions. _____, in contrast, typically provides 100% financing because it does not require the firm to make a down payment. Moreover, costs incurred to acquire the equipment, such as _____ and _____ charges, are not usually covered by a loan agreement. They may, however, be structured into a(n) _____ agreement.

5. Current financial reporting _____ for leases require that lease obligations classified as _____

leases be capitalized as a(n) _____ on the _____ sheet. A(n) _____ lease is _____ capitalized. Instead, certain information regarding such leases must be disclosed in a(n) _____ to the _____ statement. Many chief financial officers avoid _____ leases to enhance the financial image of their corporations; instead they prefer _____ leases.

6. With a(n) _____ operating lease, the lessee can avoid the risk of _____ by terminating the contract. However, the _____ of risk is not without a(n) _____ as the lease payments under such lease arrangements reflect the risk of obsolescence perceived by the lessor. At the end of the lease term, the _____ of the obsolete equipment becomes the problem of the _____. The risk of loss in residual _____ that the lessee passes on to the lessor is embodied in the _____ of the lease.

7. An advantage of leasing is that lease agreements typically do not impose financial _____ and _____ on management as does a(n) _____ agreement used to finance the purchase of equipment. The historic reason for this in _____ leases is that the _____ Service discouraged _____ leases from having attributes of _____ agreements.

8. In a properly structured _____ lease arrangement, the _____ lease payment from leasing rather than borrowing can provide a lessee with a(n) _____ cash flow. Whether the cash flow on a(n) _____ basis after taking the residual value of the equipment into account is _____ on a present value basis must be ascertained. Lease payments under a(n) _____ lease will usually have _____ impact on _____ earnings during the early years of the lease than will _____ and _____ payments associated with the purchase of the same equipment.

9. Corporate lessors may be generally categorized as _____ banks or their _____, independent _____ companies, _____ leasing subsidiary companies of nonfinance companies, _____ companies or their subsidiaries, _____ banking firms, and subsidiaries of life or casualty _____ companies.

10. Many banks and bank holding companies or their subsidiaries participate _____ in leasing through _____ relationships with independent and captive leasing companies. _____ leasing or finance companies are generally _____ of equipment manufacturers, and their primary purpose is to secure financing for the customers of the _____ company. _____ also may be involved in the _____ financing of equipment other than that manufactured by their parent company.

11. Lease _____ and financial _____ can perform a useful service for both lessees and lessors in arranging _____ leases. They can be especially helpful to a lessee by obtaining attractive _____ from a legitimate investor and advising the lessee in _____ and _____ the transaction. While lease brokers and financial advisers typically represent _____, they can be helpful to a(n) _____ in finding solutions to negotiating issues. For its services as an intermediary, the broker or adviser receives a(n) _____ commission. The amount of the remuneration depends on the _____ and _____ of the deal to the lessor in the prevailing economic _____.

12. The _____ lease provides the lessee with _____ benefits and the lessor with _____ benefits. The lease is treated as a(n) _____ sheet item and protects the lessee's _____ of acquiring the residual value of the leased equipment at the termination of the lease.

SHORT ANSWER QUESTIONS

Refer to Chapter 27, pages 883–916 in *Financial Management and Analysis*.

1. Explain how leasing works.

2. What is the ultimate form of lease financing? Why is it the ultimate form?

3. Why lease?

4. What are the accounting practices for leases?

PROBLEMS

Refer to Chapter 27, pages 883–914 in *Financial Management and Analysis.*

1. The Xhaust Company is considering the acquisition of a machine that costs $150,000 if bought today. The company can buy or lease the machine. If Xhaust buys the machine, the machine would be depreciated as a 3-year

MACRS asset and is expected to have a salvage value of $5,000 at the end of the 5-year useful life. If leased, the payments are $35,000 each year for four years, payable at the beginning of each year. The marginal tax rate for Xhaust is 30% and the cost of capital is 12%. Assume that the lease is a net lease, that any tax benefits are realized in the year of the expense, and that there is no investment tax credit.

a. Calculate the depreciation for each year in the case of the purchase of this machine.

b. Calculate the direct cash flows from leasing initially and for each of the five years.

c. Calculate the adjusted discount rate.

d. Calculate the value of the lease.

e. Calculate the amortization of the equivalent loan.

CHAPTER 28

Project Financing

FILL IN THE BLANKS

Refer to Chapter 28, pages 917–930 in *Financial Management and Analysis.*

1. _____ financing is a debt obligation that is backed by the _____ of an asset or credit support provided by a third party. The key in an asset _____ is to remove the assets (i.e., loans and receivables) from the _____ sheet of an entity. The special purpose _____ (_____) is the entity that acquires the _____ and sells the _____ to purchase the assets.

2. Structured finance is used by _____ to fund major projects. A benefit to using structured finance is that the lenders look to the cash _____ from the project being financed rather than the corporation or _____ seeking funding. This financing technique is called _____ financing and uses the _____ to accomplish its financing objectives.

3. While a(n) _____ may be willing to look initially to the cash _____ of a project as the source of funds for _____ of the loan, the lender must also feel comfortable that the loan will in fact be _____ on a(n) _____-case basis. This may involve undertakings or direct or indirect _____ by third parties who are motivated in some way to provide such guarantees.

4. The _____ party in a project is its promoter or _____. A project may have one or several _____. The motivation of _____ companies acting as sponsors is to profit in some way from the _____ or _____ of the project. The motivation of _____ companies for sponsoring a project may be simply to make a(n) _____ from selling the product produced by the project. In many instances, the motivation for the project is to provide _____ or _____ of a sponsor's basic product or to ensure a source of supply vital to the sponsor's business.

5. The ultimate goal in project financing is to arrange _____ for a project which will benefit the _____ and at the same not affect the _____ standing or _____ sheet. One way this can be accomplished is by using the credit of a(n) _____ party to support the transaction. Such a party then becomes a sponsor. However, projects are rarely financed _____ on their own merits without credit support.

6. Project _____ regard a project as acceptable only after the plant or facility has been in _____ for a sufficient period of _____ to ensure that the plant will in fact _____ the product or service at the price, in the _____, and to the standards assumed in the financial _____ that formed the basis for the financing. This _____ risk period may run from a few months to several years.

7. Project financing can sometimes be used to improve the _____ on the capital _____ in a project by _____ the investment to a greater extent than would be possible in a straight _____ financing of the project. This can be accomplished by locating other _____ interested in getting the project built, and shifting some of the _____ coverage to such parties through _____ or _____ guarantees.

8. _____ benefits from any applicable tax credits, _____ deductions, _____ deductions, _____ deductions, _____ and development tax deductions, _____-received credits, _____ tax credits, _____ gains, and noncapital start-up expenses are very significant considerations in the investment, _____ service, and cash flow of most project financings. Care must be used in structuring project financing to make sure that these tax _____ are used.

9. When a project financing is housed in a(n) _____ entity that does not have _____ to shelter, it is important to structure the project financing so that any tax benefits can be _____ to parties currently in a position to _____ such tax benefits. For U.S. federal income tax purposes, _____ control is required for tax _____, except in the case of certain _____ subsidiaries, in which _____ control may require consolidation.

SHORT ANSWER QUESTIONS

Refer to Chapter 28, pages 917–930 in *Financial Management and Analysis*.

1. Why is project financing appealing?

2. What are the credit exposures in a project financing?

3. What are some causes of project failures?

4. What is nonrecourse borrowing?

5. What are some of the incentives and disincentives of project financing?

CHAPTER 29

Strategy and Financial Planning

FILL IN THE BLANKS

Refer to Chapter 29, pages 933–967 in *Financial Management and Analysis.*

1. Budgeting is mapping out the sources and uses of funds for future periods requiring both _____ analysis, including _____, and _____. _____ analysis includes both _____ and _____ analysis to develop forecasts of future _____ and _____. _____ techniques are used as a measurement device but instead of using accounting to _____ what has happened, in budgeting, firms use accounting to _____ what we expect to happen in the future.

2. A(n) _____ advantage is the advantage one firm has over others in terms of the cost of _____ or _____ goods or services. A(n) _____ advantage is the advantage one firm has over another because of the structure of the markets (input and output

markets) in which they both operate. Only through having some type of advantage can a firm _____ in something and get _____ back in _____.

3. A(n) _____ of gaining a competitive or comparative advantage is consistent with _____ shareholder wealth. This is because projects with _____ value arise when the firm has a competitive or comparative advantage over other firms. A strategy is the direction a firm takes to meet its _____. A(n) _____ plan is how a firm intends to go in that direction. In _____ management, a strategic investment plan includes policies to seek out possible investment _____.

4. _____ forecasts are an important part of financial planning. _____ forecasts can result in shortages of _____, inadequate short-term _____ arrangements, and so on. If a firm's sales forecast _____ its mark, either _____ or _____ sales, there are many potential _____.

5. To predict _____ flows, we must forecast sales that are uncertain because they are affected by future _____, _____, and _____ conditions. Nevertheless, we can usually assign meaningful degrees of _____ to our forecasts. We forecast _____ in one of the following ways:

_____ analysis; _____ surveys; and _____ of management.

6. The experience of a firm's management and their _____ with the firm's _____, _____, and _____ make them reliable forecasters of _____ sales. The firm's own managers should have the _____ to predict the market for the goods and services and to _____ the costs of producing and marketing them. But there are potential _____ in using management forecasts. These forecasts may _____ the firm to _____ more resources, such as a larger capital budget and additional personnel, to that manager.

7. _____ is an important element in planning for both the _____-term and the _____-term. But forecasts are made by _____. Forecasters tend to be _____, which usually results in _____ than deserved forecasts of _____ sales. In addition, people tend to focus on what worked in the _____, so past successes carry more _____ in the developing forecasts than an analysis of the future. One way to avoid this is to make managers _____ for their forecasts, _____ accurate forecasts and _____ those that are way off the mark.

8. In _____, we bring together analyses of _____ flows, projected _____ statements, and projected _____ sheets. The _____ flow analyses are _____ important although generation of the _____ statement and _____ sheet is needed. Most firms extend or receive _____, so cash flows and net income do not _____.

9. A(n) _____ balance sheet is a(n) _____ balance sheet for a(n) _____ period that summarizes assets, liabilities, and equity. A pro forma _____ statement is the projected _____ statement for a future period that summarizes _____ and _____. Together, both projections help identify a firm's _____ and _____ needs.

10. The _____ of accounts method starts with the _____ budget. Before putting together the _____ income statement and balance sheet, we need to see how the various _____, _____, and _____ accounts change from month to month, based on the information provided in the cash budget. The _____ method uses historical relationships between _____ and each of the other _____ statement accounts and between _____ and each of the _____ sheet accounts.

SHORT ANSWER QUESTIONS

Refer to Chapter 29, pages 933–967 in *Financial Management and Analysis.*

1. Why is financial planning important?

2. What is the purpose of the budgeting process?

3. Explain forecasting with regression analysis.

4. How can the analysis of cash flows evaluate the performance of a firm?

5. What are the techniques used for cash flow analysis and forecasting?

PROBLEMS

Refer to Chapter 29, pages 933–967 in *Financial Management and Analysis*.

1. The financial manager of DoReMi Company has prepared the following pro forma balance sheet for next month:

Assets		Liabilities and Equities	
Cash	$500	Accounts payable	$525
Accounts receivable	300	Long-term debt	575
Inventory	300	Common equity	400
Plant and equipment	400	Total liabilities and equity	$1,500
Total assets	$1,500		

After preparing this budget, the financial manager knows that DoReMi must maintain a current ratio of 4 and a debt-to-equity ratio less than 2 at all times. How might the accounts be adjusted so that these ratios are achieved in the quickest and most correct manner? Propose an alternative pro forma balance sheet that satisfies this constraint. How does the adjustment alter DoReMi's risk?

2. Consider the Tomato Company's sales for the peak summer months:

July	$12,000
August	$20,000
September	$15,000

Eighty percent of Tomato's sales are for credit. Eighty percent of all credit sales are paid the following month and the remainder are paid two months after the sale. Estimate Tomato's cash flow from these sales.

3. Suppose a firm had the following assets at the end of 2000:

Current assets	$200,000
Plant assets	$500,000
Total assets	$700,000

If the firm had sales of $1 million, use the percentage of sales method with 2000 as the base year. What are the predicted current assets and plant assets for the firm for 2001, if sales are forecasted to be $1,400,000?

Solutions

CHAPTER 1

Introduction to Financial Management and Analysis

FILL IN THE BLANKS

Answers

1. Finance; financial management, investments, financial institutions; financial management

2. Investment decisions, financing decisions; costs, benefits; risk

3. financial analysis; divisions (or departments), product lines, creditworthiness, competition

4. Sole proprietorship, partnership, corporation; corporation, sole proprietorships; general, limited, corporation

5. articles of incorporation; bylaws; shareholders; board of directors; publicly-held, closely-held; Securities and Exchange Commission (SEC)

6. Proprietorships', partnerships', corporation; double taxation

7. limited liability company, partnership, corporation; tax, liable; joint venture; partnership, corporation

8. shareholders', price; a share of stock, shares outstanding; present value; efficient market, abnormal; risk

9. Accounting; Economic; economic

10. agent; principal; monitoring costs, bonding costs, residual loss; long; stock options, restricted stock grants

SHORT ANSWER QUESTIONS

Answers

1. No, small investors should invest in the stock market only if they are willing and able to accept more risk for the possibility of a higher return. The investor should not expect to earn a return greater than what will compensate for the risk being borne.

2. Economic profits should be the most important to the shareholder. When they are greater than zero, the shareholder is receiving adequate compensation for the investment's risk. Accounting profits may or may not compensate the shareholder since they are accounting measures and do not always reflect the risk of the investment.

3. Performance shares do not require managers to make any personal investment. The shares of stock under this plan are awards and tied to some measure of short-term accounting profits. A restricted options plan, in particular a premium-priced option, is valuable only if the price of the stock increases above its current level. This encourages managers to maximize the share price, hence, shareholder wealth.

4. Because research shows that stock markets are efficient and the information is now public, your broker should inform you that the news of the new medication has already been impounded in the price of the stock and while you cannot expect to earn abnormal returns based on this information, you are likely to earn the appropriate return to compensate for the risk associated with the investment.

5. a Because the business is a partnership, the owners' shares of the profits and losses are proportionate to what each invested. Thus for Annie, $50,000 divided by the sum of $50,000 and $25,000 = 0.667 or 2/3 of the business. For Alice, $25,000 divided by the sum of

$50,000 and $25,000 = 0.333 or 1/3 of the business. With taxable income of $12,000, Annie will declare 0.667 × $12,000 = $8,000 and Alice will declare 0.333 × $12,000 = $4,000.

b. Because both partners are jointly and severally liable for the debts of the business, creditors can recover any debt that remains after the sale of the assets by either or both partners. The assets of the firm can be sold for $30,000 and the debt amounts to $50,000, so there is $20,000 still owed to the creditors. The creditors may receive some of the $20,000 from each partner or all of the $20,000 from either partner, whoever has sufficient assets.

c. If the business had been a limited partnership, then Alice could lose only her initial investment of $25,000. She would not be held liable for any other debts. Annie would likewise lose her initial investment of $50,000 and would be liable for the $20,000 due to the creditors after the assets are sold.

d. If the business had been a corporation, then the creditors would have received the $30,000 from the sale of the assets. However, Annie and Alice would not be personally liable for the remaining $20,000 due to the creditors (unless one of them had signed a note personally guaranteeing repayment of any responsibility. This often happens when there are few owners of a corporation). In general, owners of a corporation have limited liability to the extent of the amount invested in the corporation.

CHAPTER 2

Securities and Markets

FILL IN THE BLANKS

Answers

1. security; securities market; money market, capital market, derivative; Money market; Capital market

2. Commercial paper; Treasury bill; Negotiable, commercial banks

3. Common stock; Shareholders; no; dividends; Preferred

4. principal (or face value, or par value, or maturity value); interest payments; notes; Municipal; federal; General obligation; Revenue; over-the-counter, exchanges

5. primary, secondary; private placements, underwriting

6. Exchanges; over-the-counter; privately; banks, the government; registered; Securities and Exchange

7. New York Stock Exchange; American Stock Exchange; regional, New York Stock Exchange; NASDAQ; National Market System; second; 30, 500

8. efficient, Weak, abnormal; semistrong; semistrong; Strong, insider

SHORT ANSWER QUESTIONS

Answers

1. Common stock does not have a maturity nor does it have to pay a dividend; and common shareholders are least priority in case the firm is liquidated. Bonds have a maturity date and pay an interest rate that is generally permanent. Unlike shareholders, bondholders are included among the first that are paid in the event that the firm is liquidated.

2. Because common stock does not have a maturity and the stockholders are not guaranteed to receive a dividend, they are called residual owners of the firm. For this lack of guaranteed dividend, they have the right to elect the board of directors.

   Preferred stock is more expensive than common stock and it, too, has no maturity. Preferred stockholders are guaranteed to receive dividends and have priority over common stockholders in the ownership of the firm. Unlike the common stockholders, they usually do not have voting rights.

3. Both types of bonds are municipal bonds and are free from federal taxation (i.e., the interest earned on them is free from taxation). General obligation bonds are backed by the taxing power of the issuer, whereas revenue bonds are backed by the proceeds of a specific project.

4. It all depends on a variety of factors such as the investment goals, liquidity preferences, and risk aversion of the investor. One type of investment instrument is not necessarily better than bonds or vice versa. However, there are times when one is preferred to the other in the midst of a particular business cycle, hence investors should diversify their portfolios by having a combination of stocks and bonds. If an investor is a risk taker, she or he may want only high-risk stocks. If an investor is risk averse, she or he may diversify to minimize nonsystematic risk. Further, if the investor is in a high tax bracket, bonds are more attractive than stocks that pay dividends because the interest income is not taxed at the federal rate. Likewise, an investor in a lower tax bracket may prefer dividends as they are taxed at a lower rate. Also, the need for liquidity plays a role as stocks are highly liquid and bonds have longer maturities than stocks.

5. The exchanges are a physical location where securities are traded. The over-the-counter market is not a physical location but a computerized network.

CHAPTER 3

Financial Institutions and the Cost of Money

FILL IN THE BLANKS

Answers

1. Federal Reserve System, central; monetary, loanable

2. Supply, demand, interest, borrow, interest, investing; demand, investment; supply

3. Electronic, e-cash, cybercash, digicash, electronically, Federal Reserve; cash, credit cards, checks; transaction

4. Financial institutions, financial, assets; broker, dealer, underwriting, investment portfolios

5. procuring, advice, strategies, restructuring, acquisitions

6. regulated, supervised, federal, state; legislation, Financial Services Modernization, Gramm-Leach-Bliley; underwriting, selling

7. primary, newly, securities, raise; issuer; distribute, investment bankers

8. Underwriting, Securities and Exchange; securities, registration, financial

9. good; need, pay, lend, compensated; interest rate; greater, higher, lower, lower

10. secondary, price; interest, price; face, yield, coupon

11. creditworthiness, Moody's, Standard & Poor's, Fitch; high grade; triple A; investment, noninvestment, high, junk

12. embedded, bondholder, issuer; call; retire; put; sell; convertible

13. yield, expectations, pure, liquidity, preferred habitat; segmentation

SHORT ANSWER QUESTIONS

Answers

1. Financial intermediaries can raise capital by issuing financial claims against themselves that investors purchase. The company uses the money raised to invest and technically, the investors are investing by indirect means through the financial intermediary. The investments offered provide the investor with a range of diversified investments that have various maturity dates at reduced costs.

2. There are several types of deposit institutions: commercial banks, savings and loan associations or thrifts, mutual savings banks, and credit unions.

   ■ Commercial banks: corporations owned by investors that lend to businesses and offer a multitude of basic financial services
   ■ Savings and loan associations: institutions owned by depositors that concentrate on offering home mortgage loans
   ■ Mutual savings banks: institutions owned by depositors that provide loans to the local community
   ■ Credit unions: nonprofit associations owned by depositors that make personal loans to members

3. There are a number of nondeposit financial institutions that hold financial assets:

   ■ Trust companies: act as trustee based on the terms of a contract

- Investment companies: invest in pools of assets with finances raised from the sale of stock
- Pension funds: Manage workers' retirement accumulation in stocks and bonds
- Insurers: provide a range of protection polices for the investor

4. There are many interest rates in any economy, called a structure of interest rates, and they are determined by many factors. Traditionally Treasury securities' interest rates serve as the benchmark of interest rates. The risk premium is the interest rate on a non-Treasury security and it factors in any other risks an investor may bear by buying it. These other risks include creditworthiness, option provisions, demand in the market (liquidity), the length to maturity, and tax consequences.

5. The theoretical interest rates or yields that the U.S. Treasury would pay for bonds with differing maturities are Treasury spot rates. Spot rates are also known as forward rates and some believe them to be the market's consensus of future interest rates. In this market consensus, the market prices expectations of future interest rates into the existing interest rates of investments with differing maturities. Understanding forward rates is helpful for hedging because it facilitates the use of options in order to avoid an unfavorable future interest rate.

6. The term structure of interest rates relates the yield on a bond to its maturity; the yield curve is the graph of this relationship that extends it over different maturities. The graph of the term structure can have the following shapes: a normal or upward-sloping curve, indicating the yield rises steadily as maturity increases; a downward-sloping or inverted yield curve, where yields decline as maturity increases; and a flat yield curve.

CHAPTER 4

Introduction to Derivatives

FILL IN THE BLANKS

Answers

1. futures, buy, sell, underlying; futures; settlement

2. economic, hedge, risk; Futures, exchanges, agricultural, industrial; stock, interest, currency

3. Clearinghouse, guaranteeing; Counterparty, settlement; futures

4. deposit, minimum; initial; price, fluctuates, position; market, marking, market, marking, market

5. buying, long; sale, short; buyer, profit, increases, seller, profit, decreases

6. writer, buyer, sell, price, period; premium; exercised; expiration

7. any, expiration, American; expiration, European; before, specified, Bermuda

8. intrinsic; time; economic, exercised

9. swap, periodic; dollar, notional principal; Swaps, nonfinance, interest, currency, commodity; risk, return, forward

10. cap, seller, buyer, exceeds; floor, seller, buyer, less; interest, commodity; cap, call, floor, put

SHORT ANSWER QUESTIONS

Answers

1. There are a variety of derivative instruments including futures contracts, forward contracts, option contracts, swap agreements, and cap and floor agreements. Derivative instruments are investment products that help firms to hedge against certain risks that are uninsurable. The value of the derivative comes from the basis of the contract.

2. A futures contract offers liquidation opportunities prior to the settlement date. This is achieved by the holder taking what is called an off-setting position in the same contract. The holder may also liquidate a futures contract on the settlement date. The purchaser of a futures contract receives the underlying item at the agreed-upon price. The seller liquidates the position by delivering the underlying at the agreed-upon price.

3. Forward contracts are nonstandardized, therefore terms for each contract are decided between the buyer and seller. Clearinghouses and secondary markets do not exist for forwards, therefore they are traded over-the-counter. Both futures and forward contracts provide delivery terms, however, futures contracts are not supposed to be settled by delivery as are forward contracts. Futures contracts are marked-to-market at the end of each trading day, meaning that the accounts are adjusted according to the daily closing prices. Further, this means futures accounts are allowed to have varying cash flows in and out according to price fluctuation. A forward does not have to be marked-to-market, this implies account cash flows do not vary. Finally, unlike investors in futures, investors in a forwards face credit risk exposure, or counterparty risk, since a party may default on the obligation especially since there is no clearinghouse or secondary market.

4. With an option, the buyer has the right but not the obligation to transact and the option writer must perform. In the case of a futures contract, both buyer and seller are obligated to perform. However, a futures buyer does not pay the seller to accept the obligation, while an

option buyer pays the seller an option price. The risks and rewards for the two contracts differ accordingly: Buyers of futures contracts realize a dollar-for-dollar gain (loss) when the price of the futures contract increases (decreases), and vice versa for sellers of futures contracts. Options do not have this. The most that the buyer of an option can lose is the option price at the same time they maintain all the benefits. The writer's profit is the option price, however the writer assumes much downside risk. Savvy investors use futures to protect against symmetric risk and options to protect against asymmetric risk.

5. Swaps are multiple packages of forward contracts. Because forward contracts do not have a long maturity, investors who need a longer maturity can find it in a swap. Also, swaps are convenient as the payoff for the bundle of forward contracts is negotiated together and not separately. Further, swaps have become quite liquid and there is more of a demand for them in the market.

PROBLEMS

Answers

1. The futures price of Asset X increases to $135. Alex, the buyer of the futures contract, could then sell the futures contract and realize a profit of $35 ($135 minus the futures price of $100). Effectively, at the settlement date he has agreed to buy Asset X for $100 but can sell Asset X for $135. Adrienne, the seller of the futures contract, will realize a loss of $35. If the futures price falls to $50 and Adrienne buys the contract, she realizes a profit of $50 because she agreed to sell Asset X for $100 and now can buy it for $50. Alex would realize a loss of $50. Thus, if the futures price decreases, the buyer of the futures contract realizes a loss while the seller of a futures contract realizes a profit.

2. Because it is an American call option, it may be exercised at any time up to and including the expiration date. Lydia can decide to buy from the writer of this option one unit of Asset X, for which she will pay a price of $75. If it is not beneficial for her to exercise the option, she will not. Whether the option is exercised or not, the $3 paid for the option will be kept by the option writer. If Lydia buys a put option, then she would be able to sell Asset X to the option writer for a price of $75. The maximum amount Lydia can lose is the option price. The

maximum profit that the option writer can realize is the option price. Lydia has substantial upside return potential, while the option writer has substantial downside risk. There are no margin requirements for Lydia once the option price has been paid in full. Because the option price is the maximum amount Lydia can lose, no matter how adverse the price movement of the underlying, there is no need for margin. Because the writer of an option has agreed to accept all of the risk and none of the reward of the position in the underlying, the writer is generally required to put up the option price received as margin. In addition, as price changes occur that adversely affect the writer's position, the writer is required to deposit additional margin because the position is marked to market.

3. The profit and loss from the strategy will depend on the price of Asset X at the expiration date. A number of outcomes are possible.

■ If the price of Asset X at the expiration date is less than $40 (the option price), then the investor will not exercise the option. It would be foolish to pay the option writer $60 when Asset X can be purchased in the market at a lower price. In this case, the option buyer loses the entire option price of $2. Notice, however, that this is the maximum loss that the option buyer will realize, regardless of how low Asset X's price declines.

■ If Asset X's price is equal to $40 at the expiration date, there is again no economic value in exercising the option. As in the case where the price is less than $40, the buyer of the call option will lose the entire option price, $2.

■ If Asset X's price is more than $40 but less than $42 at the expiration date, the option buyer will exercise the option. By exercising, the option buyer can purchase Asset X for $40 (the exercise price) and sell it in the market for the higher price. Suppose, for example, that Asset X's price is $41 at the expiration date. The buyer of the call option will realize a $1 gain by exercising the option. Of course, the cost of purchasing the call option was $2, so $1 is lost on this position. By failing to exercise the option, the investor loses $2 instead of only $1.

■ If Asset X's price at the expiration date is equal to $42, the investor will exercise the option. In this case, the investor breaks even, realizing a gain of $2 that offsets the cost of the option, $2.

■ If Asset X's price at the expiration date is more than $42, the investor will exercise the option and realize a profit. For example, if the price is $50, exercising the option will generate a profit on Asset X of $10. Reducing this gain by the cost of the option ($2), the investor will realize a net profit from this position of $8.

4. The intrinsic value is $110 – 100 = $10. That is, an option buyer exercising the option and simultaneously selling the underlying asset would realize $110 from the sale of the underlying, which would be covered by acquiring the underlying from the option writer for $100, thereby netting a $10 gain. This option is "in the money." When the exercise price of a call option exceeds the current price of the underlying, the call option is out-of-the money and has no intrinsic value. If the exercise price is equal to the current price it is at-the-money and also has no intrinsic value (0).

For a put option, the intrinsic value is equal to the amount by which the current price of the underlying is below the exercise price: $100 – 90 = $10. The buyer of the put option who exercises the put option and simultaneously sells the underlying will net $10 by exercising. The asset will be sold to the writer for $100 and purchased in the market for $90. For the put option, it would be: in-the-money when the price of the underlying is less than exercise price, out-of-the money when the current price exceeds the exercise price, and at-the-money when the exercise price is equal to the current price.

5. Consider a corn farmer and a canning company that uses the corn in the operation of its business. The concern of the farmer is that the price of corn will decline, thereby forcing him (or her) to sell his corn at a lower price. The concern of the canning company is that the price of corn will increase, resulting in a rise in its production costs. Consider first the farmer; suppose the corn will be available at a time when the farmer can sell a corn futures contract to deliver corn for $X per bushel. The number of bushels expected to be sold will determine how many bushels of corn the farmer will seek to deliver. By selling futures, the farmer has locked in a price of $X per bushel. Consequently, even if the price of corn is $X – 2 per bushel, the farmer will receive $X per bushel. If instead, the price of corn is $X + 2 per bushel, the farmer has given up the opportunity to benefit from a higher price because he has agreed to accept $X per bushel.

Now let's look at the canner. By buying a corn futures contract, the canner can assure that the price at which it must purchase corn will be no higher than $X per bushel. So, if corn increases to $X + 2 per bushel, the canner only needs to pay $X per bushel. In contrast, if the price of corn decreases to $X – 2 per bushel, the canner gave up the opportunity to benefit from a lower cost for corn.

CHAPTER 5

Taxation

FILL IN THE BLANKS

Answers

1. Congress, legislation, Internal Revenue Code; Internal Revenue Service (IRS), interprets, adds, implements; IRS, providing, processing, collecting, explaining, rulings

2. income tax, 1909, simple, complex; analyst, today, future; after, performance, changing

3. marginal, defines, bracket, dollar; average, ratio, paid; progressive, average, higher; investment, financing, taxable, marginal

4. shareholders, dividends, twice, corporate, shareholders', corporation, third; triple, dividends-received; recipient, dividends, dividend, taxable; dividends-received, increases, return, investing

5. accelerated, straight-line; depreciation, rate, physical, effect, income; uniformity, depreciation, taxpayers, calculations, accelerated, shorter

6. capital gain, realized, sold, paid; treatment, lower, tax

7. Investment, ITC, stimulate, reducing, computed; ITC, reinstated, Congress, spending; credits, deductions, reduce, deduction, indirectly

8. net operating loss, deductions, income; back, preceding, forward, future, reduce; back, forward

9. worldwide, income; Nonresident, seat, management, corporate; tax, no, minimal; havens

SHORT ANSWER QUESTIONS

Answers

1. The following are the main kinds of taxes:

   ■ Income taxes are taxes based on the amount of income earned.
   ■ Employment taxes are also based on wage and salary income and paid by both the employee and employer for Social Security, Medicare, and retirement.
   ■ Excise taxes are a simple way of augmenting revenue by charging tax on certain commodities such as alcoholic beverages, tobacco products, telephone service, and gasoline.
   ■ Import and export taxes, also known as tariffs, are taxes from trading with foreign countries.

2. Investors receive a tax break on dividend income. Because of this, investors require a lower return on these types of securities which means the cost of capital is lower for the firm that issued the securities. A firm's dividend income is not taxed, whereas interest income is taxed like any other income. Dividends paid by a firm are not deductible, whereas interest paid by a firm is fully deductible. The tax treatment of dividends and interest influences the financial decision-making because of its affect on the cost of capital.

3. The modified accelerated cost recovery system (MACRS), has four features:

   ■ The depreciation rate used each year is either 150% or 200% of the straight-line rate, depending on the type of property, applied against the undepreciated cost of the asset.
   ■ The salvage value of the asset is ignored, so the depreciable cost is the original cost and the asset's value is depreciated to zero.
   ■ A half-year of depreciation is taken in the year the asset is acquired, no matter whether it is owned for one day or 365 days.

■ The depreciation method is switched to the straight-line method when straight-line depreciation produces a higher depreciation expense than the accelerated method.

Because the MACRS is an accelerated method, depreciation expenses are greater sooner, thus reducing taxable income and tax rates when compared to straight-line. Straight-line depreciation is acceptable in cases where firms may not be able to make the best use of quicker depreciation that is offered by MACRS. Some companies use both methods, MACRS for tax purposes and straight-line for financial reporting purposes. This results in a difference in taxable income and may create deferred tax liabilities.

4. Taxes are of great concern because tax rates change often and the financial analyst needs to consider this dynamic tax environment when making an evaluation of a firm's future cash flows. Understanding foreign and domestic tax rates provides more accurate analyses and insight into the corporation's decision making process. Along with taxes, depreciation rates are very important to consider, despite the fact that they are not a cash flow. Depreciation still influences a firm's taxes by reducing taxable income, which is a cash flow.

PROBLEMS

Answers

1. a. Using straight-line depreciation method: The depreciation allowance is $56,000/7 = $8,000 per year. Recall that only half can be taken the first year with the remainder taken at the end, so the depreciation schedule is as follows:

Year	Depreciation Allowance
1	$4,000
2–7	$8,000
8	$4,000

b. Using MACRS depreciation method, the depreciation schedule is as follows:

Year	Depreciation Allowance
1	$56,000(0.1429) = $8,002.40
2	$56,000(0.2449) = 13,714.40
3	$56,000(0.1749) = 9,794.40
4	$56,000(0.1249) = 6,994.40
5	$56,000(0.0893) = 5,000.80
6	$56,000(0.0892) = 4,995.20
7	$56,000(0.0893) = 5,000.80
8	$56,000(0.0446) = 2,497.60

2. Depreciation tax shield is the product of the depreciation expense and the tax rate:

Year	Depreciation Expense	Depreciation Tax Shield
1	$8,002.40	$2,400.72
2	13,714.40	4,114.32
3	9,794.40	2,938.32
4	6,994.40	2,098.32
5	5,000.80	1,500.24
6	4,995.20	1,498.56
7	5,000.80	1,500.24
8	2,497.60	749.28
Total	$56,000.00	$16,800.00

3.

Income from operations:	$4,000,000
plus 20% of dividend income:	100,000
Taxable income	$4,100,000
Tax liability = Taxable income × Tax rate =	$4,100,000 (0.35)
	= $1,435,000

4. Application of net operating loss to prior years' taxable income results in a refund of $507,500:

Years	Refigured Taxable Income	Refigured Tax	Refund of Prior Taxes Paid	Amount of Loss Applied
1998	$0	$0	$0	$0
1999	0	0	245,000	700,000
2000	0	0	175,000	500,000
2001	0	0	87,500	250,000
Total			$507,500	$1,450,000

Total refund is $270,000.

$550,000 may be carried over to future taxable income because a total of $1,450,000 of the $2,000,000 loss is applied against 1999, 2000, and 2001 taxable income.

CHAPTER 6

Financial Statements

FILL IN THE BLANKS

Answers

1. Financial, operating, financing, investment; information, investors, creditors, assess, earnings, cash, earnings

2. data, financial, management, generally accepted accounting principles, GAAP; balance, condition, position, assets, liabilities, equity, fiscal, historical

3. balance, assets, future, inflows, liabilities, creditors, outflows, equity, shareholders', stockholders', ownership

4. Liabilities, current, long-term, deferred; operating, one; Accounts, accrued, current portion, short-term; Long-term, beyond; notes, bonds, capital lease, pension

5. Equity, interest; common, preferred; book value, equity; sum, retained, common, preferred, historical

6. Preferred, preferred, stock, balance sheet; remainder, common; common, paid-in, retained

7. income, summary, revenues, expenses; profit, loss, operating, financing

8. cash flows, cash, operating, investment, financing; cash flows, operating, investing, financing; selling, assets, issuing, securities, operations

9. operations, indirectly; investing, financing; investing, investments, disposal, acquisitions, divestitures; financing, sale, repurchase, stock, issuing, retirement, debt, payment, dividends

10. equity, shareholders', equity; balance, income, analyst, equity; balance, number, shareholders' equity, exercise, options, repurchased

SHORT ANSWER QUESTIONS

Answers

1. The financial statements are created based on assumptions that affect the use and interpretation of financial data:

   ■ Transactions are recorded at historical cost so values reported in statements are not market or replacement values.
   ■ The dollar is the unit of measure.
   ■ The statements are recorded for specified periods of time such as fiscal year or quarter. Fiscal year end is usually chosen to coincide with the firm's lowest amount of operating cycle activity.
   ■ Accrual accounting and the matching principle are used to prepare statements. This means income and revenues are matched in timing such that income is recorded in the period in which it is earned and expenses are reported in the period in which they are incurred.
   ■ Firms are expected to always be a going concern.
   ■ Full disclosure requires providing more information than what is reported on the financial statements.
   ■ Statements are to be prepared and interpreted conservatively.

2. The two major categories of assets are current assets and noncurrent assets. Current assets are those assets that will be used or converted to cash in one year or one operating cycle and noncurrent assets are assets such as plant assets, intangibles, and investments.

3. Intangible assets are long-term investments and are the current value of nonphysical assets. Examples of intangible assets are:

■ A patent that gives the exclusive right to produce and sell a particular asset

■ A copyright that gives the exclusive right to publish and sell a literary, artistic, or musical composition

■ Goodwill that is created when one company buys another company at a premium

4. Four different labels are applied to the number of shares of a corporation on a balance sheet:

■ The number of shares authorized by shareholders

■ The number of shares issued and sold, which can be less than those authorized by shareholders

■ The number of shares currently outstanding, which can be less than the number of shares issued if the corporation has repurchased some of its issued stock or has sold less than what is authorized

■ The number of shares of treasury stock, that is, repurchased stock

5. Through the analysis of individual cash flows, investors and creditors can examine the following characteristics of a business:

■ Whether financing is internally or externally generated

■ Whether the firm is able to cover all debt obligations

■ Whether the firm is able to afford expansion

■ Whether the firm is able to pay dividends

■ Whether the firm has financial flexibility

PROBLEMS

Answers

1.

Cash	$15,000	Accounts payable	$34,000
Inventory	27,500	Notes payable	3,000
Gross plant and equipment	50,000	Long-term debt	26,000
Accumulated depreciation	17,500	Common equity	12,000
Net plant and equipment	32,500		
Total assets	$75,000	Total liabilities and equity	$75,000

Solution requires using the following relationships:

- Total assets = Total liabilities and equity
- Gross plant and equipment – Accumulated depreciation = Net plant and equipment
- Current assets + Net plant and equipment = Total assets
- Current liabilities + Notes payable + Long-term debt + Common equity = Total liabilities and equity

2. | | |
    |---|---:|
    | Earnings before taxes | $45,000 |
    | Less: taxes (30% of $45,000) | 13,500 |
    | Net income | $31,500 |
    | Preferred stock dividends | 20,000 |
    | Earnings available for common shareholders | $11,500 |
    | Common stock dividends (40% of $11,500) | 4,600 |
    | Retained earnings | $6,900 |

3.

Statement of Cash Flows

Cash flow from operations

Net income	$64,000	
Increase in current assets	–22,000	
Decrease in current liabilities	+30,000	
Depreciation	+60,000	
Net cash flow from operations		$152,000

Cash flow from investing activities

Purchase plant and equipment	–$58,000	
Net cash flow from investing activities		–58,000

Cash flow from financing activities

Issue long-term debt	+15,000	
Repurchase of common stock	–45,000	
Dividends on common stock	–10,000	
Net cash flow from financing activities		–40,000
Net cash flow		$54,000

Mathematics of Finance

FILL IN THE BLANKS

Answers

1. time value, cash, different; future, valuable, today, invested, interest; compounding, discounting

2. lend, present; require, paid, future; future, present, interest; interest, use, length, time, risk, borrowed, repaid

3. basic, $PV(1 + i)^N$, present, future, future, present; interest, compounding; interest, interest, interest

4. financial, patterns, cash, perpetuities, annuity, deferred; timing; Tables, present value, future value, present, annuity, future, annuity

5. series, cash, cash, sum, present, future; equal, periodic

6. perpetual, ordinary; ordinary, end; level, beginning, annuity due

7. deferred, equal, after, period; deferred, present, ordinary, discounted, earlier

SHORT ANSWER QUESTIONS

Answers

1. A dollar is worth less today than a dollar some time in the future if that dollar is invested such that it earns interest in the future. A dollar is worth more today than a dollar some time in the future if that dollar has no investment opportunity. If the dollar is not invested, no investment opportunities can come to pass. The value the dollar holds is in its liquidity, which gives the investor the flexibility to invest the dollar when a future opportunity arises.

2. The comparison of alternative financing or investment opportunities is difficult when interest rates do not have comparable terms. In order for comparisons to be done, the rates must be converted to a common unit. Two ways to convert interest rates stated over different time intervals into a common measure are to use the annual percentage rate (APR) and the effective annual interest rate (EAR). Annualizing the rates is an easy conversion and simplifies the comparison. The annualized rate is the stated rate of interest per compound period times the number of compounding periods in a year.

   ■ The APR ignores compounding, thus understating the true annual rate of interest when the interest is compounded before the year's end.
   ■ The effective annual rate (EAR) is the true economic return for a given time period because it accounts for compounding of interest. This form is the most useful to compare interest rates.

CHAPTER 7 PROBLEMS

Answers

1. Given:

   r = 7.5% or 0.075
   PV = \$500

   Solve: FV for different values of t

a. $\$500(1 + 0.075)^1 = \$500(1.0750) = \quad \$537.50$

b. $\$500(1 + 0.075)^5 = \$500(1.4356) = \quad \$717.80$

c. $\$500(1 + 0.075)^{10} = \$500(2.0610) = \$1,030.50$

2. Given:

$r \quad = 7.5\%$ or 0.075
$FV = \$500$

Solve: PV for different values of t

a. $\$500\dfrac{1}{(1 + 0.075)^1} = \$500(0.9302) = \quad \$465.10$

b. $\$500\dfrac{1}{(1 + 0.075)^5} = \$500(0.6966) = \quad \$348.30$

c. $\$500\dfrac{1}{(1 + 0.075)^{10}} = \$500(0.4852) = \$242.60$

3. Given:

$r \quad = 4.5\%$ or 0.045
$PV \quad = \$1,000$

Solve: FV for a variety of different interest scenarios
a. $\$1,000(1 + 0.045)^3 = \$1,000(1.1412) = \$1,141.20$

b. Total interest earned $= \$1,141.20 - 1,000 = \$141.20$

c. If Natalie would have withdrawn all her interest each year, she would have earned $\$1,000 \times 0.045 = \$45$ interest each year. For the three years, she would have earned $3 \times \$45 = \$135$.

4. Since growth rate = annual interest rate = average annual return, use the basic valuation equation and solve for the rate that doubles every dollar he invests.

$$FV = PV(i+r)^t \Rightarrow \$2 = \$1(1+r)^5 \Rightarrow \frac{\$2}{\$1} = (1+r)^5$$

$$\Rightarrow r = \sqrt[5]{\frac{\$2}{\$1}} - 1 \Rightarrow r = 0.1487 = 14.87\%$$

5. Given:

$$r = 5\% \text{ or } 0.05$$
$$PV = \$4,000$$
$$FV = \$4,000 + 2,000 = \$6,000$$

$$FV = PV(i+r)^t \Rightarrow \$6,000 = \$4,000(1+0.05)^t \Rightarrow \frac{3}{2} = (1.05)^t$$

$$\Rightarrow \frac{\ln(3/2)}{\ln(1.05)} = t \Rightarrow t = 8.31 \text{ years}$$

6. To accurately compare these quotes, convert them all to EAR.

   Bank A: EAR $= (1 + \frac{0.145}{1})^1 - 1 = 14.5\%$ because it is already compounded annually.

   Bank B: EAR $= (1 + \frac{0.14}{12})^{12} - 1 = 14.93\%$

   Friend: EAR $= e^{0.1375} - 1 = 14.74\%$

   Bank A provides the better rate.

7. APR $= 2.9\% \times 12$ months $= 34.8\%$

   EAR $= (1 + \frac{0.348}{12})^{12} - 1 = 40.92\%$

   Because the customer is actually paying 40.92% on unpaid balances, it might be in the customer's best interest to transfer the balance to a credit card charging a lower interest rate or to pay off the credit card altogether and ask for a lower interest rate.

8. Given:

$r \quad = 10\%$
$CF_0 = \$150$
$CF_1 = \$300$
$CF_2 = \$225$
$CF_3 = \$410$

Solve: FV at end of third period

$FV = \$150(1+0.10)^3 + \$300(1+0.10)^2 + \$225(1+0.10)^1 + \$410(1+0.10)^0$
$= \$199.65 + \$363 + \$247.50 + \$410$
$= \$1,220.15$

9. Given:

$CF_1 = \$2,500$
$CF_2 = \$3,000$
$CF_3 = \$5,000$
$CF_4 = -\$2,500$
$r \quad = 12\%$

Solve: PV as of the end of period 0

$$PV = \frac{\$2,500}{(1+0.12)^1} + \frac{\$3,000}{(1+0.12)^2} + \frac{\$5,000}{(1+0.12)^3} - \frac{\$2,500}{(1+0.12)^4}$$
$$= \$2,232.14 + 2,391.58 + 3,558.90 - 1,588.76$$
$$= \$6,593.86$$

10. Given:

$CF = \$2,400,000$
$T \quad = 20$
$r \quad = 10\%$

Solve: PV of annuity due

$$PV = \$2,400,000 + \$2,400,000 \sum_{t=1}^{19} \frac{1}{(1+0.10)^t}$$
$$= \$2,400,000 + \$2,400,000(8.3649)$$
$$= \$2,400,000 + \$20,075,760 = \$22,475,760$$

11. Given:

CF = $20,000
T = 4 (deferred 8 years)
r = 7%

Solve: PV of deferred annuity

$$PV = \$20,000 \left(\sum_{t=1}^{4} \frac{1}{(1+0.07)^t} \right) \left(\frac{1}{(1+0.07)^8} \right)$$

$= \$20,000(3.3872)(0.5820)$
$= \$39,427.01$

Principles of Asset Valuation and Investment Returns

FILL IN THE BLANKS

Answers

1. financial, good, bad; good, increase, bad, won't; good, bad, benefits, outweigh, costs; best, financial, financed

2. discount, capitalization, translate, present; discount, pay, right; return, requires, price, expected; single, series, series, perpetual, present, amount, timing, discount

3. averse, risk; higher, uncertain; Buyers, sellers, buy, sell, profitable; over-, under-; balance, equilibrium

4. price, highest; restrictions, buying, selling; limit, costs, highest

5. inverse, value, discount, higher, discount, lower, value, lower, discount, higher, value

6. return, benefit; change, value, appreciation, depreciation, flow, dividend, interest, both, flow, value

7. return, yield; return, yield, annual, average; return, internal, IRR; average, geometric, arithmetic, compounding

8. discount, cost, future, internal; internal, inflows, same, internal

9. effective, compounding; reinvested, different, modified internal, MIRR

SHORT ANSWER QUESTIONS

Answers

1. The reason for the inverse relation between the discount rate applied to future cash flows from an investment and the value of the investment today can be explained mathematically taking into consideration the basic valuation formula for future value and present value. When the present value is calculated, the discount rate assumes its position in the denominator of the formula with the future value in the numerator. The larger the discount rate, the larger the denominator, which in turn results in a smaller value after dividing the numerator by the denominator, hence a smaller present value. The smaller the discount rate, the smaller the denominator, which in turn results in a larger value after dividing the numerator by the denominator, hence a larger present value. For a direct application of this question, see problem one in the Problems section.

2. The investor must consider his or her personal level of risk aversion which is represented by the discount rate. Risk averse investors avoid risky investments regardless of the chance of receiving higher returns.

   Timing and frequency of future cash flows also are important. Taken with the discount rate, they will influence the decision on whether to make the investment. If potential investments have similar risks and cash flows, then increased frequency of cash flows indicates the preferred investment. When investments have dissimilar risks, then the present value of each investment should be examined in order to chose the preferred investment.

3. The average annual return is the geometric average annual return. Unlike the arithmetic annual return, the geometric average annual return includes compounding when calculating the rate of return. The arithmetic average annual return calculates a flat constant return rate because it does not incorporate the interest on interest that is earned. The preferred annual return is the one that incorporates compounding, hence the geometric average allows for more precise assessment.

PROBLEMS

Answers

1. While the answer is intuitive, the step-by-step solutions should clarify the mathematics of the problem:

   Using the 5% discount rate: $PV = \dfrac{\$500}{(1 + 0.05)^1} = \$476.19$

   Using the 6% discount rate: $PV = \dfrac{\$500}{(1 + 0.06)^1} = \$471.70$

   Note: Compare the denominators. Because 1.05 is less than 1.06, this indicates that the result from dividing the future value by 1.05 will yield a higher value than dividing by 1.06. This higher value translates into a higher present value, or up-front cost that Karen must pay for the investment. Depending on Karen's available funds that she now has to invest, she is better off investing at the higher discount rate because she will be required to pay less for it up front than if she chooses the lower rate. Knowledge of the actual future value and actual discount rates are unnecessary as long as one knows the same future value is being divided by two discount rates, one larger than the other.

2. This investment involves perpetual cash flows. Therefore,

$$PV = \frac{\$1,500}{0.10} = \$15,000$$

   ■ If the investor pays more than $15,000, then less than 10% is earned.
   ■ If the investor pays less than $15,000, then more than 10% is earned.
   ■ If the investor pay $15,000, the investor earns 10%.

3. Given:

   $PV = \$3,000$
   $FV = \$5,500$

CF = none
N = 4 years

Solve: The average annual return on the investment, i
Using a financial calculator: $i = 16.36\%$
Or

$$\$5,500 = \$3,000(1 + i)^4$$
$$i = \sqrt[4]{\frac{\$5,500}{\$3,000}} - 1 = 16.36\%$$

4. a. Given:

PV = \$100,000
CF_1 = \$20,000
CF_2 = \$40.000
CF_3 = \$25,000
CF_4 = \$35,000

Solve: i
Using a financial calculator, $i = 7.31\%$.

b.

$$PV = \frac{\$20,000}{(1+0.10)} + \frac{\$40,000}{(1+0.10)^2} + \frac{\$25,000}{(1+0.10)^3} + \frac{\$35,000}{(1+0.10)^4}$$
$$= \$135,758.17$$

5. a. $FV = \$25,000(1 + 0.08) + \$27,000(1 + 0.12) + \$31,050(1 + 0.15)$

Or $FV = (((\$25,000(1.08))(1.12))(1.15))$

$FV = \$34,776$ at the end of the third year.

b. $i = \sqrt[3]{\frac{\$34,776}{\$25,000}} - 1 = 11.63\%$ per year

CHAPTER 9

Valuation of Securities and Options

FILL IN THE BLANKS

Answers

1. common, ownership; Shares, perpetual, maturity; Owners, right, dividends, guaranteed; dividends, constant, constant

2. Notes, bonds, interest, semiannually, principal, face; percentage; constant, straight, zero, maturity

3. Dividend Valuation, DVM, value, stock, dividend, constant, constant; value, share, dividend, difference, required, return, growth, dividends; required, return, stock, dividend, capital; growth, dividend, lower, greater, greater, less, reinvest, lower

4. dividends, constant, value, present, dividends, period, perpetuity; required, return, RRR, compensate, time value, uncertainty, future, flows

5. Opportunity, earned, alternative, similar; minimum, required, return, discount, time value, risk; dividend, price, grow, capital; capital, taxes, taxes, capital, sold

6. bonds, value, coupon, yield; coupon, yield, more, maturity, premium; coupon, yield, less, discount; coupon, valued

7. right, buy, sell; not, stock, exchange, traded; buy, call; buy, exercise, strike, expiration; sell, put

8. convertible, stock, investor; straight, without, stock; Callable, issuer, buy, investor, price, call, prior, convertible, callable

SHORT ANSWER QUESTIONS

Answers

1. If a bond's present value is greater than its maturity value, it sells at a premium because investors will pay more for a bond if it pays more than the going rate for bonds of similar risk. If the bond's present value is equal to its maturity value, then the bond sells at par. If the bond sells below its maturity value, it is trading at a discount because investors are not going to pay the maturity value for a bond that pays less than the going rate.

2. All three types of securities are valued by the present value of all future cash flows expected to be received. With shares of common stock, the value is equal to the present value of all dividends expected to be received from that share. As mentioned previously, common stock has no maturity so the value is the present value of an infinite stream of dividends. One catch is that the dividends are neither fixed nor guaranteed. Thus, the value of preferred stock is likewise the present value of all future dividends and the dividends are guaranteed. The value of a debt security is the present value of the sum of the present value of the interest payments and the present value of the maturity value.

3. The factors that affect the time value of an option are the value of the underlying asset, the exercise price, the time value of money, the expected volatility in the value of the underlying asset, and the time to maturity.

4. The Dividend Valuation Model is a formula that values a share of stock that either pays a constant dividend or that pays dividends that grow at a constant rate. The model states that the value of a share of stock is equal to the ratio of next period's dividend to the difference between the required rate of return and the growth rate of dividends.

It is useful and flexible, especially for dividends that have changing rates over time. Its meaning is intuitive—as the current dividend increases, the value of the stock increases, and in turn, if uncertainty increases, then the discount rate increases, which decreases the value of the stock.

5. The yield-to-maturity differs from the yield-to-call in that the number of periods for which the cash flows are discounted back is the number of periods to the expected call date and the call price of the bond is discounted back instead of the face value of the bond.

PROBLEMS

Answers

1. The price of the bond will increase because the cash flows (coupon payments) are discounted at a lower rate. This increases the present value which is evident in the increased price of the bond.

2. Yes. According to the option, the investor has one month to decide to purchase 1,000 shares of XYZ Company for $30 per share plus the option cost, which translates into $1.50 more per share. Therefore the cost to the investor is $31.50 per share. Because the current price is $1 higher than the option price, the investor could exercise this option and then sell the shares in the open market for a profit of $1 per share. The investor can exercise the option at any time up until and including the expiration date. Therefore if the price of the stock falls, the option will not be exercised and the investor will lose his $1,500. If the investor thinks the stock will rise and wants more than $1 per share profit, he should exercise the option immediately and hold the stock until it rises to what he considers an acceptable level.

3. ABC preferred stock $\rightarrow r = \dfrac{\text{dividend}}{\text{price}} = \dfrac{\$3.45}{\$35} = 9.86\%$

Because the return on this investment is less than the required 10%, the investment would not be made.

4.

$$\text{Price} = \$11 \sum_{t=1}^{3} \frac{1}{(1.08)^t} + \$125 \left(\frac{1}{(1.08)^3} \right)$$

$$= \$28.35 + \$99.23 = \$127.58$$

This investment should only be taken if the investors required rate of return is less than 8%. The current price is $130, which is greater than the price at which it will be called, $127.58, so the investor will not receive the 8% annual return on the investment.

5. The cash flows are as follows:

$$
\begin{aligned}
D_1 &= D_0(1 + 0.02) = 2.25(1.02) = \$2.30 \\
D_2 &= D_1(1 + 0.02) = 2.30(1.02) = \$2.35 \\
D_3 &= D_2(1 + 0.02) = 2.35(1.02) = \$2.39 \\
D_4 &= \$2.39 \\
D_5 &= \$2.39
\end{aligned}
$$

Since the third year begins the perpetuity:

$$\text{Price} = \frac{\$2.39}{0.16} = \$14.94$$

Therefore, the price per share for the stock that has this particular cash flow of dividends is:

$$\text{Price} = \frac{\$2.30}{1.16} + \frac{\$2.35}{(1.16)^2} + \frac{\$2.39}{(1.16)^3} + \frac{\$14.94}{(1.16)^3} = \$17.25$$

6. The bond pays $60 every six months for ten periods. It will pay $1,000 at maturity. The effective annual yield is 14% so the appropriate semiannual rate to discount the cash flows is 7%.

$$\text{Price} = \$60 \sum_{t=1}^{10} \frac{1}{(1.07)^t} + \$1,000 \frac{1}{(1.07)^{10}}$$

$$= \$456.53 + \$508.40 = \$964.93$$

Because the investor is holding the bond to maturity, the average annual yield is the yield to maturity on the bond, which is 14%.

7. Assume the interest is paid at the end of the year, then:

$$\text{Return} = \frac{\text{Ending price} - \text{Beginning price} + \text{Interest}}{\text{Beginning price}}$$

$$= \frac{\$1,037.50 - 1,000 + 93.75}{\$1,000}$$

$$= 13.125\%$$

$$\text{Coupon yield} = \frac{\text{Interest}}{\text{Price}} = \frac{\$93.75}{\$1,000} = 9.375\%$$

$$\text{Capital yield} = \frac{\$1,037.50 - 1,000}{\$1,000} = 3.75\%$$

8. The entire yield is the capital yield: $\$1,000 = \$738.75(1 + r)^{15}$
   Solving algebraically for the rate:

$$r = \sqrt[8]{\frac{\$1,000}{\$638.75}} - 1 = 5.76\%$$

9. The round trip transactions cost of $\$10.99 \times 2$ must be considered in the return calculation:

$$\text{Return} = \frac{\text{Sell price} - \text{Buy price}}{\text{Buy price}}$$

$$= \frac{(1,000 \times 8.625 - 10.99) - (1,000 \times 5 + 10.99)}{(1,000 \times 5 + 10.99)}$$

$$= \frac{\$8,614.01 - 5,010.99}{5,010.99}$$

$$= 71.9\%$$

10.

$$\$1,080 = \sum_{t=1}^{8} \frac{50}{(1+r)^t} + \frac{\$1,000 + 100}{(1+r)^8}$$

Using a financial calculator: $r = 4.82\%$ for six months. To find the effective annual yield to call:

$$\begin{aligned}
\text{EAR} &= (1 + \text{Interest rate per period})^{\text{periods per year}} - 1 \\
&= (1.0482)^2 - 1 \\
&= 9.87\%
\end{aligned}$$

CHAPTER 10

Risk and Expected Return

FILL IN THE BLANKS

Answers

1. uncertainty, knows, tax, demand, economy, interest; risk, uncertainty; Uncertainty, knowing; Risk, uncertainty, greater, uncertainty, greater, risk

2. Cash, sales, operating, financial; Sales, uncertainty, units, good, price; Operating, variable, fixed; Financial, financing

3. debt, interest, principal, payments, bondholders, owners; cash, debt, default, credit; default, debt

4. Reinvestment, reinvesting; yields, reinvest, interest, bond, return; yield, coupon, longer, more, more, reinvest; yield, time, maturity, greater, more, value

5. Interest, sensitivity, value, interest; Market, rate, discount, present, discount

6. Purchasing, price level; borrows, long, coupon, increases, benefits, increase, creditor, cheaper

7. Currency, domestic, foreign, value, future; Currency, cash, currency

8. Risk, dislike; averse, avoid; neutral; neutral, compensation, risk; preference, affinity

9. Diversification, vary, same, same; returns, correlated; tendency; returns, positively, same, negatively, opposite; uncorrelated, no

10. Risk, add, unsystematic, company; Risk, assets, market, systematic

11. William Sharpe, return, risk, assets; capital, pricing, CAPM; CAPM, return, asset, return, risk-free, risk; return, compensation, value, premium, compensation, risk; diversified, risk, assets, nondiversifiable, market, systematic

12. CAPM, risk, return, arbitrage, model, APM, Stephen Ross; APM, asset, identical, different, identically; returns, compensate, risk, risk, economic, company; theoretical, pricing, factor

SHORT ANSWER QUESTIONS

Answers

1. The degree of operating leverage (DOL) is the ratio of the percentage change in operating cash flows to the percentage change in units sold. The degree of financial leverage (DFL) is the ratio of the percentage change in cash flows to the owners to the percentage change in operating cash flows. The degree of total leverage (DTL) is the product of DOL and DFL. DTL measures the sensitivity of the cash flows to owners to changes in unit sales.

   The degree of operating leverage measures the sensitivity of operating cash flows to changes in sales and the degree of financial leverage measures the sensitivity of owners' cash flows to changes in operating cash flows. The combination is the degree of total leverage.

2. Default may result from many types of failures. Some examples are:

   ■ Failure to make interest or principal payments
   ■ Failure to make sinking fund payments
   ■ Failure to meet conditions of the loan
   ■ Bankruptcy

Financial managers are concerned about their own default because if there is a perception of lack of creditworthiness, then the firm's cost of capital increases. Likewise, if the managers invest in another firm's debt, they are risking their firm's funds. Default risk is comprised of sales risk, operating risk, and financial risk.

3. Prepayment risk and call risk are related to reinvestment risk. The rule to remember is that the greater the risk (i.e., cash flows), the greater the return.

   ■ Prepayment risk is associated with loans that have a schedule for the repayment of principal with the right to repay without penalty prior to the end of the loan. The risk comes in when the interest rate falls below that of the loan; then the investor is paying more for the loan than initially contracted.
   ■ Call risk is the risk that an issuer will call an investment product that has a callable option. Investors are compensated for this risk with a premium. However if the issue is called, then the investor must find another investment mechanism.

4. If an investor plans to hold a bond until its maturity, then the value is stable despite the changing interest rates. However, if the investor does not want to hold the bond to maturity, then the value is directly affected by the changing interest rates. As interest rates fall, bond values rise and vice versa, so if an investor plans to get rid of a bond, it needs to be done during times of low interest rates.

   For a specific maturity and if the rate on the coupon is relatively great, then the bond's value is not subject to much change in the yield because the greater cash flows are not as affected by the discount rate. However if the bond has a longer maturity, then the bond's value is more affected.

5. Expected returns are a measure of future returns without delineating all the possible outcomes. The more the possible outcomes (range), the greater the risk. The standard deviation is a measure of the dispersion of risk which indicates the likelihood of all possible outcomes. The variance is the square of the standard deviation and has the same meaning as standard deviation. It is often referred to as the volatility.

PROBLEMS

Answers

1. a. DOL at 10,000 units $= \dfrac{10,000(\$1,500 - 30)}{10,000(\$1,500 - 30) - \$175,000} = 1.01$

   b. DFL at 10,000 units $= \dfrac{10,000(\$1,500 - 30) - \$175,000}{10,000(\$1,500 - 30) - \$175,000 - \$65,000}$

   $= 1.00$

   c. DTL at 10,000 units $=$ DOL $\times$ DFL

   $= 1.01 \times 1.00 = 1.01$

   d. $Q_{BE} = \dfrac{\$175,000 + \$65,000}{(\$1,500 - 30)} = 164$ units

   e. The sales volume is increased by 5,000 units, which indicates a 50% increase in units sold. Therefore, DTL $\times$ 50% = 1.01 $\times$ 50% = 50.5% increase in the cash flows available to owners.

2. a.

   Investment 1: expected value $=$ \$1,075
   Investment 2: expected value $=$ \$1,075

   b.

   Investment 1: standard deviation $=$ \$278
   Investment 2: standard deviation $=$ \$388

   Investment 1:

$p_n x_n$	$p_n(x_n - E(x))^{2*}$	
\$500	213,906	
400	14,063	
175	115,719	
$E(x) =$ \$1,075	343,688	$\sigma(x) =$ \$586.25

Investment 2:

$p_n x_n$	$p_n(x_n - E(x))^2$ [a]	
$375	45,156	
400	14,063	
300*	16,633	
$E(x) =$ $1,075	75,852	$\sigma(x) = 275.41

[a] Actual value is rounded appropriately.

c. *Investment 1 is riskier.* Investment 1 provides the same expected return, but has a higher standard deviation than Investment 2.

3. a. $r_f = 6\%$ $r_m - r_f = 4\%$

Security	Expected Return
A	$6\% + 0.85(4\%) = 9.4\%$
B	$6\% + 1.00(4\%) = 10\%$
C	$6\% + 1.25(4\%) = 11\%$
D	$6\% + 1.50(4\%) = 12\%$

b. $B_p = \dfrac{0.85 + 1.00 + 1.25 + 1.50}{4} = 1.15$

c. $r_p = \dfrac{0.094 + 0.10 + 0.11 + 0.12}{4} = 0.106$ or 10.6%

4. a. The covariance between Investment 1 and 2:

$$E(x)_{Inv1} = 0.15(0.18) + 0.30(0.50) + 0.55(0.40) = 0.397$$

$\sigma(x)_{Inv1}$
$$= \sqrt{0.15(0.18 - 0.397)^2 + 0.30(0.50 - 0.397)^2 + 0.55(0.40 - 0.397)}$$
$$= 0.1012$$

$$E(x)_{Inv2} = 0.15(0.25) + 0.30(0.45) + 0.55(0.30) = 0.3375$$

$\sigma(x)_{\text{Inv2}}$

$= \sqrt{0.15(0.15 - 0.3375)^2 + 0.30(0.45 - 0.3375)^2 + 0.55(0.30 - 0.3375)}$

$= 0.0992$

$$\begin{aligned} \text{Covariance} = \ & 0.15(0.18 - 0.397)(0.15 - 0.3375) \\ & + 0.30(0.50 - 0.397)(0.45 - 0.3375) \\ & + 0.55(0.40 - 0.397)(0.30 - 0.3375) \\ = \ & 0.0095 \end{aligned}$$

b. The correlation coefficient $= \dfrac{\sigma_{1,2}}{\sigma_1 \sigma_2} = \dfrac{0.0095}{(0.1012)(0.0992)} = 0.9395.$

c. Because the covariance is positive, the investment's returns covary together in the same direction. The correlation coefficient, which is positive and close to 1, means that the two investments tend to go in the same direction at the same time together.

CHAPTER 11

The Cost of Capital

FILL IN THE BLANKS

Answers

1. cost, capital, funds; borrowed, cost, interest; equity, cost, return, appreciation, dividends; capital, required, return

2. structure, debt, preferred, common; optimum proportions, capital

3. cost, debt, dollar, marginal, rate, tax, taxable; interest, taxable, effective, lower

4. debt, stock, flotation; payments, lawyers, accountants, bankers; all-in-cost, up

5. cost, preferred, dollar, issuing, preferred; Preferred, maturity; maturity, perpetual preferred

6. cost, common, common, internally, externally; Internally, retained, externally, shares, common

7. Dividend Valuation, DVM, common, price, stock, present, future, dividends, discounted, required, return, equity; dividends, constant, future

8. Capital Asset Pricing, CAPM, diversified, market; compensated, time, money, risk; compensation, time, money, risk premium, market, beta.

9. optimal capital, maximize, investment, marginal, capital, equal, benefit; optimal capital budget, expenditure, marginal, capital, internal, efficiency

SHORT ANSWER QUESTIONS

Answers

1. The cost of capital and the required rate of return are similar. The difference comes in from the perspective. Cost of capital is from the firm's perspective as it is the amount the firm has to compensate investors in order to receive their money. Required rate of return is from the investor's perspective as it represents the personal return rate they require in order to temporarily part with their money and invest it in the company. These are marginal concepts because they represent the incremental cost or return associated with raising or investing an additional dollar.

2. The cost of capital is determined in three steps:

   ■ Calculate the proportions of each source of capital to be used.
   ■ Calculate the cost of each source of capital.
   ■ Calculate the weighted average cost of capital using these two measures.

3. It is appropriate to use the DVM when companies have stable dividend policies. The CAPM relies on historical values for stock returns and market returns and should be reserved for only publicly traded firms. A pitfall of this model is often the lack of data and even if data is available, the past is not indicative of future earnings.

PROBLEMS

Answers

1. Yield on current debt:

$$\$900 = \sum_{t=1}^{10} \frac{\$35}{(1+r)^t} + \frac{\$1,000}{(1+r)^{10}}$$

$$r = 4.7813\%$$

Effective annual yield $= (1 + 0.047813)^2 - 1 = 9.79\%$

After-tax effective yield: $r_d^* = 9.79\%(1 - 0.30) = 6.85\%$

2. Without flotation costs: $r_p = \dfrac{\$1.05}{\$35} = 3.00\%$

With flotation costs: $r_p = \dfrac{\$1.05}{\$35(1-0.01)} = \dfrac{\$1.05}{\$34.65} = 3.03\%$

3. Given:

$$D_0 = \$3.12$$
$$P = \$65$$
$$g = 5\%$$

$$r_e = \frac{\$3.12(1 + 0.05)}{\$65} + 5\%$$
$$= 5.04\% + 5\% = 10.04\%$$

4. Given:

$$r_f = 4\%$$
$$r_m = 11\%$$
$$B = 1.35$$

$$r_e = 4\% + 1.35(11\% - 4\%)$$
$$= 4\% + 9.45\% = 13.45\%$$

5. Estimation of the cost of capital for Sutton, Inc.:

Given:

$$
\begin{aligned}
r_d &= 8\% \\
D_p &= \$2.00 \\
P_p &= \$30 \\
P &= \$25 \\
D_1 &= \$1.50 \\
g &= 5\% \\
t &= 40\%
\end{aligned}
$$

Solve: Cost of capital (r_w) for alternative financing proportions

Calculation of costs of sources of funds:

Cost of debt $\quad\quad\quad\quad\quad r_d^* = 0.08(1 - 0.40) = 0.08(0.6) = 0.048$

Cost of preferred equity $\quad r_p = \dfrac{\$2.00}{\$30.00} = 0.0667$

Cost of common equity $\quad r_e = \left(\dfrac{\$1.50}{\$25.00}\right) + 0.05$

$$= 0.06 + 0.05 = 0.11$$

Financing arrangement #1:

$$
\begin{aligned}
r_w &= [0.30(0.048)] + [0.10(0.0667)] + [0.60(0.11)] \\
&= 0.0144 + 0.00667 + 0.066 \\
&= 0.087 \text{ or } 8.7\%
\end{aligned}
$$

Financing arrangement #2:

$$
\begin{aligned}
r_w &= [0.50(0.048)] + [0.25(0.0667)] + [0.25(0.11)] \\
&= 0.024 + 0.016675 + 0.0275 \\
&= 0.0682 \text{ or } 6.82\%
\end{aligned}
$$

CHAPTER 12

Capital Budgeting: Cash Flows

FILL IN THE BLANKS

Answers

1. objective, wealth; investment, value; invest, tangible, intangible, income, cash, reinvest, pay

2. Capital, assets, notes, bonds, stock, short-term; capital, projects; factors, estimate, future, change, uncertainty, future

3. risk, sales, operating; Sales, uncertainty, sold, price, operating, uncertainty, operating, mix, operating; business, discount, return, capital, required, cost

4. budgeting, identifying, selecting, long, benefits, one; budgeting, ongoing; budgeting, strategy, objectives

5. length, risk, dependence; economic, useful, length, benefits; risk, nature; dependence, independent, mutually exclusive, contingent, complementary

6. difference, with, without, incremental; change, components, operating, investment, expenditures, acquire, disposing

7. simplest, outflow, acquired, inflow, outflow, economic; revenues, expenditures, taxes, working; operating

8. depreciation, depreciation tax-shield; outflow, inflow; accelerated, straight-line; accelerated, larger, sooner, straight-line

9. Salvage, not, depreciation; guess, asset, worth, useful; Salvage, dispose

SHORT ANSWER QUESTIONS

Answers

1. The five stages of the capital budgeting process are:

   ■ Stage 1: Investment screening and selection. A project's cash flows are screened and selected according to their ability to fulfill corporate strategy.
   ■ Stage 2: Capital budget proposal. A capital budget is proposed for the selected projects.
   ■ Stage 3: Budgeting approval and authorization. Projects that are approved are included in the capital budget. More analysis is conducted prior to making expenditures.
   ■ Stage 4: Project tracking. Projects that are approved are tracked during the life of the project.
   ■ Stage 5: Postcompletion audit. Projects that are approved are audited from time to time in order to review if they still comply with corporate strategy.

2. The use of current assets are usually the focus of short-term investment decisions and don't necessarily entail long-term cash flow projections. Current assets are cash, marketable securities, accounts receivable, and inventory. With long-term investment decisions, cash flow projections are necessary as there is a concern for the time value of money and the day-to-day operating needs of the firm. A firm needs both current and long-term assets in order to function even during down times.

3. A firm must consider future cash flows and how these cash flows influence the assets already utilized by the firm. New projects may or may not adversely affect the current assets in place. Often, firms can take on additional projects if they already have the necessary assets in place. When decisions are made, capital rationing is a concern as a

company may not be able to financially take on all the projects it wants.

- An independent project is as the name implies, a project that does not rely on another project. Hence their cash flows are unrelated.
- Mutually exclusive projects are projects in which the cash flows affect each other. In other words, the firm can either do one project or the other, but not both.
- Contingent projects rely on the acceptance of another project.
- Complementary projects are projects that positively influence other projects.

4. Cash flows from investments come from asset acquisition, asset disposition, taxes, and operations. All these cash flows include costs of assets, expenditures in the utilization and disposal of the assets, and the effect of taxes.

PROBLEMS

Answers

1. Asset acquisition cash flow for Year 0 = ($10,000) for the cost of the asset.
Operating Cash Flows for Year 1 through Year 5 = $5,500 each year.
Asset disposition cash flow = $0 as there is no salvage value.

Operating Cash Flows

Change in revenues	$15,000
Less change in expenses	−8,000
Change in before-tax cash flow	$7,000
Less change in depreciation	−2,000
Change in taxable income	$5,000
Less change in taxes	−1,500 ⇨ 30% of $5,000
Change in net income	$3,500
Plus change in depreciation	+2,000
Change in after-tax cash flow	$5,500

2. Asset acquisition cash flow for Year 0 = ($49,000) for the cost of the asset. Operating Cash Flows for Year 1 through Year 7 = $5,500 each year. Asset disposition cash flow = $7,500.

Operating Cash Flows

Change in revenues	$18,000
Less change in expenses	−5,000
Change in before-tax cash flow	$13,000
Less change in depreciation	−7,000
Change in taxable income	$6,000
Less change in taxes	−1,500 ⇨ 25% of $6,000
Change in net income	$4,500
Plus change in depreciation	+7,000
Change in after-tax cash flow	$11,500

Asset Disposition

Cash inflow from sale of cookie press	$10,000
Tax on sale of press	−2,500
Net cash flow form asset disposition	$7,500

3. Asset acquisition cash flow for Year 0 = ($30,000) for the asset. Operating Cash Flows for Year 1 through Year 7 = $3,300 each year. Asset disposition cash flow = $5,500.

Asset Acquisition

Cost of equipment	$(20,000)
Installation	(8,000)
Spare parts inventory	(2,000)
Initial investment outlay	$(30,000)

Operating Cash Flows

Change in revenues	$0
Less change in expenses	−3,000
Change in before-tax cash flow	$3,000
Less change in depreciation	−4,000 ⇨ $28,000/7
Change in taxable income	$(1,000)
Less change in taxes	−300 ⇨ tax savings
Change in net income	$(700)
Plus change in depreciation	+4,000
Change in after-tax cash flow	$3,300

Asset Disposition

Salvage value	$5,000
Tax on salvage value	−1,500
Net cash flow form asset disposition	$5,500

CHAPTER 13

Capital Budgeting Techniques

FILL IN THE BLANKS

Answers

1. cost, pay, finance; cost, explicit, interest, implicit, price, common, return, suppliers, capital, value, risk; uncertain, greater

2. payback, length, money; initial, outflow, inflows, initial, outflow; payback, payoff, recovery

3. discounted payback, pay, original, discounted, payback, longer, discounted, cash, discounted

4. Net present, NPV, expected; net, difference, change; changes, inflows, investment, outflows, NPV, difference, inflows, outflows

5. NPV, future, time value, risk, future; NPV, maximize; NPV, determine, changes, profitability

6. investment, NPV, NPV, discount; investment, graphical, NPV, discount; NPV, range, discount

7. profitability index, PI, operating, inflows, investment, outflows; PI, benefit-cost, benefit, cost; PI

8. internal rate, IRR, discount, future, zero, IRR, discount, NPV, $0; IRR, yield; mutually exclusive, IRR, not

SHORT ANSWER QUESTIONS

Answers

1. The six capital budgeting techniques are:

   ◼ Payback period
   ◼ Discounted payback period
   ◼ Net present value (NPV)
   ◼ Profitability index (PI)
   ◼ Internal rate of return (IRR)
   ◼ Modified internal rate of return (MIRR)

   When evaluating investment projects, the ones chosen should always maximize owner wealth. To determine if they will maximize shareholder wealth or not, cash flows, and their uncertainty from each investment should be estimated.

2. Payback and discounted payback periods:

   ◼ The sooner the payback, the better.

   Net present value:

   ◼ NPV > 0 indicates the investment increases shareholder wealth—accept the project.
   ◼ NPV < 0 indicates the investment decreases shareholder wealth—reject the project.
   ◼ NPV = 0 indicates the investment does nothing to change shareholder wealth—indifferent about the project.

   Profitability index:

   ◼ PI > 1 indicates the investment returns more—accept the project.
   ◼ PI < 1 indicates the investment returns less—reject the project
   ◼ PI = 1 indicates the investment returns nothing extra but loses nothing—indifferent about the project.

   Internal rate of return:

   ◼ IRR > cost of capital indicates the investment is expected to return more—accept the project.

- IRR < cost of capital indicates the investment is expected to return less—reject the project.
- IRR = cost of capital indicates the investment is expected to return what is required—indifferent about the project.

Modified internal rate of return:

- MIRR > cost of capital indicates the investment is expected to return more—accept the project.
- MIRR < cost of capital indicates the investment is expected to return less—reject the project.
- MIRR = cost of capital indicates the investment is expected to return what is required—indifferent about accepting or rejecting the project.

3. The profitability index is a good evaluation technique. It considers a variety of factors such as all cash flows, the time value of money, the risk associated with these, and capital rationing. However, the PI is not foolproof. If projects require differing amounts to be invested at different times, then the PI may not coincide with NPV. Also, mutually exclusive projects are not comparable using PI.

4. In a sense, the IRR is the discount rate that breaks even. It makes the present value of all expected future cash flows equal to zero assuming these cash flows are reinvested at the same IRR each time. The MIRR technique is much more realistic because it assumes that the reinvested rates vary. A drawback to IRR and MIRR is that while they consider all cash flows and their timing, they do not directly take risk into account. Risk is indirectly accounted for when using the measures in the actual act of discounting. Selection of IRR and MIRR should be taken cautiously as capital rationing and status (dependence, independence, mutual exclusivity) of a project influence the selection.

5. When selecting the appropriate techniques, it is important to remember that discounted cash flows are preferred to the nondiscounted cash flow techniques although they may not necessarily be appropriate for all situations (although they are appropriate for most). The goal is to always maximize shareholder wealth.

- If projects are independent and capital rationing is of no concern, then any of the discounted cash flow techniques are appropriate.

■ Recall that for mutually exclusive projects, the NPV method leads to investing in projects that maximize wealth and if the capital budget is limited, the NPV and PI methods should be used.

■ If the projects are so constrained that they are mutually exclusive, cost the same amount to start, and have similar risk, then use either NPV or MIRR.

■ If projects are mutually exclusive with different risks and scales, then NPV should be used over MIRR. If capital rationing is necessary, then the NPV or PI are appropriate.

■ Overall, NPV should guide project selection; in particular, NPV of the entire capital budget is the real concern.

In practice, more than one technique is used in order to give a more rounded view of the project. As mentioned above, discounted cash flow techniques (NPV, IRR, PI) are used as a primary method and payback period is used as a secondary method. IRR with NPV is being used more frequently.

PROBLEMS

Answers

1. You are the manager and are considering the following two projects for investment:

	Year 0	Year 1	Year 2	Year 3
Project A	($10,000)	$3,000	$7,000	$9,000
Project B	($5,000)	$3,000	$4,000	$5,000

a. Project A takes two years in order to regain the initial investment of $10,000.

Project B takes two years in order to regain the initial investment of $5,000.

b.

Discounted Cash Flows

Project A

Year 1 $3,000[1/(1 + 1/10)] = $2,727

Year 2 $7,000[1/(1 + 1/10)^2] = $5,785

Year 3 $9,000[1/(1 + 1/10)^3] = $6,762

Project B

Year 1 $3,000[1/(1 + 1/10)] = $2,727

Year 2 $4,000[1/(1 + 1/10)^2] = $3,306

Year 3 $5,000[1/(1 + 1/10)^3] = $3.757

Project A takes three years in order to regain the initial investment of $10,000.

Project B takes two years in order to regain the initial investment of $5,000.

As a manager, you like the fact that the initial outlay for project B will be paid back quickly, however, this does not necessarily indicate that project B is the best project. If the required return or cost of capital was higher than 10%, then the discounted cash flow would have been a lesser amount and it would take longer to recoup the initial outlays for both investments.

c. NPV for project A = $2,727 + $5,785 + $6,762 = $15,274

NPV for project B = $2,727 + $3,306 + $3,757 = $9,790

Both projects produce positive NPV, which is desirable of all projects.

d. PI for project A = $\dfrac{PV \text{ cash inflows}}{PV \text{ cash outflows}}$ = 1.5274

PI for project B = $\dfrac{PV \text{ cash inflows}}{PV \text{ cash outflows}}$ = $\dfrac{\$9,790}{\$5,000}$ = 1.958

The PIs indicate that for project A, for every $1 outflow, there is approximately $1.53 inflow and for project B, for every $1 outflow, there is approximately $1.96 inflow. It is necessary for cash inflow to be greater than cash outflow in order for a project to be considered.

e. IRR for project A =

$$\frac{\$3,000}{(1 + IRR)} + \frac{\$4,000}{(1 + IRR)^2} + \frac{\$5,000}{(1 + IRR)^3} - \$10,000 = 0$$

Using a calculator or trial and error, IRR for project A = 33.24%.
    IRR for project B =

$$\frac{\$3,000}{(1 + IRR)} + \frac{\$4,000}{(1 + IRR)^2} + \frac{\$5,000}{(1 + IRR)^3} - \$5,000 = 0$$

Using a calculator or trial and error, IRR for project B = 54.05%.
    The IRR indicates the discount rate that would generate an NPV
of $0. It also reflects the assumption that cash flows are reinvested at
the IRR rate. These rates are not necessarily realistic as investments
that produce those types of returns would have to be very risky.

  f. For project A:

$$FV = \$3,000(1.10)^2 + \$7,000(1.10) + \$9,000(1.10)^0 = \$20,330$$

$$PV = \$10,000$$

$$FV = PV(1 + MIRR)^t$$

$$\$20,330 = \$10,000(1 + MIRR)^t$$

$$(1 + MIRR)^3 = 2.033$$

$$MIRR = \sqrt[3]{2.033} - 1 = 26.68\%$$

For project B:

$$FV = \$3,000(1.10)^2 + \$4,000(1.10) + \$5,000(1.10)^0 = \$13,330$$

$$PV = \$5,000$$

$$FV = PV(1 + MIRR)^t$$

$$\$13,330 = \$5,000(1 + MIRR)^3$$

$$(1 + MIRR)^3 = 2.666$$

$$MIRR = \sqrt[3]{2.666} - 1 = 38.66\%$$

The MIRRs reflect a more realistic rate of reinvestment of cash flows. While these rates are high, they are not as high as IRR. Still, in today's market, while these types of investments with these returns are possible, they would indicate risky investments.

g. If both projects are independent, then both should be undertaken because they both have positive NPVs. This means they will both increase the value of the firm.

h. If the projects are mutually exclusive, then project A should be undertaken because it increases the value of the firm more than project B. In particular, project A increases the value of the firm by $5,274 whereas project B only increases the value of the firm by $4,790.

CHAPTER 14

Capital Budgeting and Risk

FILL IN THE BLANKS

Answers

1. investment, industry; economic, market, taxes, interest, international

2. uncertainty, future, evaluating; opportunity, earn, same, risk; return, capital, additional, compensate, risk

3. risk, projects, total, standalone; assets, standalone, relevant; portfolio, returns, correlated; addition, portfolio, risk, portfolio

4. statistical, risk, project's, range, standard deviation, coefficient, variation; dispersion, greater, uncertainty

5. sensitivity, change, reestimating, scenarios; Sensitivity, scenario, what-if, outcomes, one

6. Simulation, two, more, same; computer, probability, outcomes, probability, variable, change; simulations, internal rates, frequency, return

7. option pricing, real, real options, ROV, beyond, net present value, supplemented, options; options, abandon, exercised, expand, defer, future; strategic, revised, strategic

8. valuation, Black-Scholes; Black-Scholes, five, valuation; sensitive, difficult, volatility, two, strategic, volatility, value, cost, capital, static

9. certainty, certain, equivalent, risky; certainty, approach, risk, separates, value, risk, period's, risk, preferences, incorporated; net present, interpreted, reliable, period's

10. single, capital, risks; applying, discounted, budgeting, rejection, overdiscounting, acceptance, underdiscounted

SHORT ANSWER QUESTIONS

Answers

1. The range is a statistical measure that represents the distance between the two extreme outcomes of the probability distribution and is calculated as the difference between the best and the worst (largest and smallest) possible outcomes. The wider the range, the further apart are the two extreme possible outcomes, therefore implying increase in risk.

    The standard deviation measures each possible outcome's deviation or difference from the expected value and the likelihood the outcome will occur. The larger the standard deviation, the greater the dispersion and, hence, the greater the risk.

    Comparison is not feasible between standard deviations of different projects' cash flows if they have different expected values, thus the coefficient of variation translates the standard deviation of different probability distributions into a comparable measure. The coefficient of variation for a probability distribution is the ratio of its standard deviation to its expected value.

2. Sensitivity analysis illustrates the effects of changes in assumptions by changing one factor at a time. While this is helpful when isolating one factor, it is not very realistic when trying to view the effects of many factors changing during the life of a project. If the change of more than one variable at a time is desired, then simulation analysis is the analysis to use.

    Simulation analysis is more realistic than sensitivity analysis because it projects for many variables simultaneously. This method should only be used with a computer as it is computationally expensive. Simulation analysis examines a project's total risk with generations of multiple scenarios. This is useful for the project, but not useful for the owner's portfolio, meaning that simulation analysis does not take into account the toll of the project's risk on the portfolio. When studying a project's risk, its effect on the total risk of the other projects and the firm as a whole is necessary.

3. Financial leverage is debt obligation carried by the firm. In particular, it is the structured interest and principal payments that the firm must pay. The more debt a firm carries, the more financial leverage it has. Thus, the firm carries more risk because these debt obligations must be met. However, given the hierarchy of payoffs, if a firm is liquidated, debt holders receive their portion prior to equity holders. Therefore, debt financing increases the firm's risk of equity but for the debt holding investor, it is a less risky investment compared to the equity holder.

4. When a firm wants to take on a new project for which it has no experience, the best way for that firm to gauge risk is to find a firm that is a pure play. A pure play is a firm whose only line of business is the one of interest to the firm looking to take on a similar project. In this manner, the firm can use the pure play firm as a model for how they might implement the project and assess the project's risk. The assessment of risk is a proxy from the pure play firm. The investigating firm may use the pure play firm's market beta in order to estimate the project's risk.

5. The cost of capital is the amount the firm must pay creditors and investors in order to receive their investment in the company. In other words, it is how much the investors require in order to forgo use of their cash. Therefore the investors require adequate compensation for the time value of money and the probability of receiving these cash flows from the firm. To estimate the cost of capital, the cost of debt, preferred stock, and common stock are weighted and added to yield the weighted average cost of capital (WACC). This gives management an overall picture of their total costs to investors in order to receive their investment based on the risk of the project and investors' risk aversion level.

PROBLEMS

Answers

1.

$$B_{asset} = B_{equity}\left[\dfrac{1}{1 + \dfrac{(1 - \text{marginal tax rate})\text{debt}}{\text{equity}}}\right] = 1.05$$

(This is the beta to be used for the estimate of the project risk.)

Required rate of return = Risk free rate + B(market risk premium)
= 5.5 + 1.05(12)
= 18.1%

Because ABC's cost of capital is 15% and the required rate of return on this project is 18.1%, ABC should invest in this project. If the required rate of return were equal to the cost of capital, then ABC would technically break even and if the required rate of return for this project were less than the cost of capital, ABC would not invest in the project as it would not cover cost of capital.

2. a. The cash flow range for each project are:

R_A = Best possible outcome – Worst possible outcome
= $1,300 – $800 = $400

R_B = Best possible outcome – Worst possible outcome
= $3,00 – $1,500 = $1,500

b. The expected cash flows for each project are:

$$E(x_A) = \sum_{n=1}^{N} x_n p_n$$
$$= 0.25(\$1,300) + 0.40(\$1,500) + 0.35(\$800)$$
$$= \$1,205$$

$$E(x_B) = \sum_{n=1}^{N} x_n p_n$$
$$= 0.30(\$3,000) + 0.25(-\$1,000) + 0.45(\$1,500)$$
$$= \$1,325$$

c. The standard deviation of the possible cash flows for each project are:

$$\sigma(x_A) = \sqrt{\sum_{n=1}^{N} P_n[x_n - E(x)]^2}$$
$$= \sqrt{0.25(1,300-1,205)^2 + 0.40(1,500-1,205)^2 + 0.35(1,300-1,205)^2}$$
$$= \sqrt{\$40,225} = \$200.56$$

$$\sigma(x_B) = \sqrt{\sum_{n=1}^{N} P_n[x_n - E(x)]^2}$$
$$= \sqrt{0.30(3,000-1,325)^2 + 0.25(-1,000-1,325)^2 + 0.45(1,500-1,325)^2}$$
$$= \sqrt{\$2,296,875} = \$1,485.56$$

d.

$$\text{Coefficient of variation for Project A} = \frac{\text{Standard deviation}}{\text{Expected value}}$$
$$= \frac{\$200.56}{\$1,205} = 0.16644$$

$$\text{Coefficient of variation for Project B} = \frac{\text{Standard deviation}}{\text{Expected value}}$$
$$= \frac{\$1,485.56}{\$1,325} = 1.1212$$

e. Using NPV analysis:

$$\text{NPV}_A = \$1,205 \sum_{t=1}^{5} \frac{1}{(1.13)^t} - \$2,000 = \$2,238$$

$$\text{NPV}_B = \$1,325 \sum_{t=1}^{5} \frac{1}{(1.18)^t} - \$1,000 = \$3,144$$

Because the projects are mutually exclusive, Project B should be chosen. Note the higher expected return for the higher expected risk that Project B carries (see NPV, standard deviation, and coefficient of variation).

f.

$$\text{NPV}_{B1} = \$1,325 \sum_{t=1}^{5} \frac{1}{(1.19)^t} - \$1,000 = \$3,051$$

$$\text{NPV}_{B2} = \$1,325 \sum_{t=1}^{5} \frac{1}{(1.18)^t} - \$1,800 = \$2,344$$

$$\text{NPV}_{B3} = \$1,000 \sum_{t=1}^{5} \frac{1}{(1.18)^t} - \$1,000 = \$2,127$$

$$\text{NPV}_{B4} = \$1,000 \sum_{t=1}^{5} \frac{1}{(1.19)^t} - \$1,800 = \$1,258$$

CHAPTER 15

Intermediate and Long-Term Debt

FILL IN THE BLANKS

Answers

1. loan, principal, end, intervals; lender, bondholder, interest; interest, end; fixed, variable, floating

2. property, secured, security, collateral; ability, payments, unsecured, debenture

3. Term, borrower, creditor, creditor, bank, insurance, finance; Term, maturity, fixed, fixed, demand

4. registered, bearer; registered, records, interest, principal, registered; bearer, possession, certificate, payment; interest, bearer, coupon, cashes

5. conversion, exchange, security, common stock; bondholder, attractive; price, increases

6. analyze, rate, default, rating; Moody's Investors, Standard & Poor's, Fitch; credit, cost, marketability; restricted, minimum; risk, greater, default, credit, greater, greater

7. rating, high, low, high; investment-grade, prime, A, B; Noninvestment-grade, B, speculative, high-yield, junk.

8. Rating, credit, character, capacity, collateral, covenants; Character, ethical, quality; Capacity, repay; assets, value, quality; Covenants, terms, conditions

9. funds, bond, lowest, retire, fall; highest, lowest, sell; debt; derivative, synthetically, fixed, floating, interest, currency, commodity, stock index

SHORT ANSWER QUESTIONS

Answers

1. On debt obligations, the interest rate is calculated by the interest rate reset formula which makes use of the floating rate. The floating rate is found by adding the reference rate that is specified in the contract, and the quoted margin that is fixed over the debt's term. These rates do have collars, meaning that they have maximums and minimums.

2. Term loans are repaid in installments either monthly, quarterly, semi-annually, or annually according to an amortized schedule.

   An interest-only loan means just that, no principal payments are made until the end of the term. What is paid according to a schedule are the interest payments. This kind of loan is also called a bullet loan because the last payment that includes the principal is a killer.

3. Both are debt obligations, also called certificates of indebtedness. They obligate the borrower to repay the amount borrowed, with interest, in a scheduled fashion. The difference between the two is that a bond has an indenture agreement indicating the rights and obligations of the borrower while a note does not. The indenture agreements also provide for a trustee to oversee the borrowing for the benefit of the bondholder. The note is a less formal agreement.

4. The basic features a bond issue are:

   ■ Denomination: par, face, or maturity value (i.e., the amount of the debt)
   ■ Term to maturity: the length of the life of the bond
   ■ Interest: the amount of the coupon paid per year
   ■ Security: some bonds are backed by collateral, others aren't

■ Seniority: there is a seniority ranking
■ Retirement: through the use of trust funds, call, and put options
■ Convertibility: also use call and put options

5. A bond issuer may retire debt by either calling it before it reaches its maturity date or paying off a portion of it by buying it back from the bondholder. The process of retiring the debt through repurchase may either happen with individual investors or in the market place.

   Bonds are retired before maturity date if the current interest on the debt is lower than the debt they are paying. This means that they can get debt at a cheaper price than what they are now paying for it. Bonds may also be retired in order to improve the firm's debt rating. If the firm has too many bonds or too many bonds that are low grade, then retiring some of that debt will lessen their default rate. The issuer could also retire debt because they may not be receiving adequate tax deductions or they may need to generate funds.

6. A convertible bond has a provision built in so that the bondholder may exchange the bond issue for shares of stock. A warrant is the right to buy the common stock at the exercise price. It gives the bondholder the opportunity to buy the shares of stock and maintain possession of the bond. Detachable warrants may be separated from the debt and traded.

PROBLEMS

Answers

1. Zero-coupon bonds would have more of a change in price because they are subject to more interest rate risk. A zero-coupon bond's entire cash flow is not received until maturity. Therefore, for the length of that maturity, its value is influenced by interest rate movements. The greater the coupon rate, the higher the price, which is calculated from cash flows that are received earlier and at regular intervals, than the zero-coupon bond. Therefore, the 8% coupon bond would not be as influenced by the interest rate changes and thus has less interest rate risk than the zero-coupon bond.

   Likewise, because the 8% coupon bond has more frequent cash flows, this in turn means that it has greater reinvestment risk than the zero-coupon bond. The investor must find adequate investments frequently to reinvest the 8% coupon's interest payments, but the investor has to find an alternative investment for the zero-coupon payoff just once.

2. a. The conversion price of the bond is the ratio of the face value of the bond to the price of a share of the common stock.

$$\text{Conversion price} = \frac{\$1,000}{45} = \$22.22$$

b. The bond's market conversion price is the market value of the stock times the number of shares that can be exchanged.

$$\text{Market conversion price} = \$35 \times 45 = \$1,575$$

c. The effective conversion price is the price that is paid for each share of common stock when the bond is converted.

$$\text{Effective conversion price} = \frac{\$1,575}{45} = \$35$$

d. If the investor converts the bond into the shares, she or he will receive stock worth $1,575. However if the investor accepts the call, she will receive $1,800. The investor should accept the call. She would only convert the shares if the call price of the bond was less than $1,575.

3. a. If the current market price is $33 and the warrant entitles you to pay only $20 a share, you should be willing to pay $13 (the difference) for the warrant.

b. Because there are five years until expiration, this will make the warrant more valuable as the stock has several years to increase in value. In essence, you will be paying a lower market value for the stock because of the warrant option.

4. a. The semiannual interest payments are: 5% × 12 million = $600,000. There will be 16 payments in eight years and the maturity value of $12 million will be received in the 16th period so the market value of the bonds is the present value of the expected future cash flows:

$$\text{Market value} = \$600,000 \sum_{t=1}^{16} \frac{1}{(1.03)^t} + \$12,000,000 \frac{1}{(1.03)^{16}}$$
$$= \$7,536,661.22 + \$7,478,003.27 = \$15,014,664.49$$

b. If KLH calls the bonds, it will pay 5% above the initial $20 million, which equals $12,600,000. If it buys the bonds on the open market, the premium on these bonds is tax deductible: $15,014,664,49 − 12,000,000 = $3,014,661.49 and it will cost the company 0.75 × $3,014,661.49 = $2,260,996.12 after taxes. Therefore, it would cost KLH $2,260,996.12 + $12,000,000 = $14,260,996.12 to buy the bonds on the open market.

KLH should exercise the call. It would only cost the firm $12,600,000 versus buying the bonds on the open market for $14,260,996.12. If the bonds were callable at a higher price (for example: $125), this would turn the tables and make it more cost effective for KLH to purchase bonds on the open market (because in this case the call would cost KLH $15,000,000).

5. a. The present value of the bond is $875 and the future value in two years is $1,000. There are no other payments made because it is a zero-coupon bond, so the interest rate is:

$$\$1,000 = \$875(1+r)^2$$
$$r = \sqrt{\frac{\$1,000}{\$875}} - 1$$
$$r = 6.9\%$$

b. The deductible interest expense per year is:

For year 1 = 0.069 × $875 = $60.38

For year 2 = 0.069($875 + $60.38) = $64.54

Common Stock

FILL IN THE BLANKS

Answers

1. stock; common, preferred; shares, certificates; shareholders, stockholders; return, dividends, cash

2. common; liability, shares, ownership, classified, voting, buy

3. shares, authorized; not; issued, actually, fewer, authorized; left, outstanding, issued; retired, treasury

4. Common, elect, directors, vote, merger, authorize, vote, amendments; classes, votes, percentages; controlling, retain

5. Cumulative, minority; cumulative, accumulate, pile, seats, governance, smaller

6. one, entire; classified, staggered; advantage, continuity; experienced, one year

7. additional, common, rights, rights, existing, maintain, holding

8. directors, dividend, obligation; cash; shares, property

9. reinvest, shares, dividend, DRP, shareholders, dividends, additional, cash; additional, outstanding, issued

10. split; divides, existing, more, portion, same; reverse, raises, reducing

11. dividend, decision, cash; no, growth, payout, low regular, periodic; Irrelevance, Bird, Tax-Preference, Signaling, Agency

12. repurchasing, cash, taxes; Cash, ordinary; repurchase, capital, price; higher, gains, lower

SHORT ANSWER QUESTIONS

Answers

1. Shareholders do not actually purchase a piece of the company per se, instead they buy the right to future income and are allowed to be involved in the firm's activities and decision making.

2. Preferred stockholders are given preference over common stockholders. This means that the company must give income to the preferred shareholders before the common shareholders. The same is true of dividends. Also, while dividends are not guaranteed to common shareholders, they are to preferred shareholders. Common shareholders have voting rights, whereas preferred shareholders do not. However, only when firms halt dividend payment, can preferred shareholders receive some temporary voting rights.

3. Common equity is created through residual ownership in a firm. This residual ownership is created by issuing shares of stock, protecting and maintaining of the firms earnings, and reinvesting of earnings back into the firm, meeting creditor obligations, and paying any required dividends to preferred shareholders. Any remaining earnings may either be kept by the firm or paid out to common shareholders in the form of dividends.

4. A publicly held corporation is one whose shares of stock are traded in financial markets. Publicly held firms are subject to scrutiny and must meet the disclosure requirements set forth by the SEC. Because of this scrutiny and disclosure, public firms can raise outside capital easier than other types of firms because they are fairly transparent.

   A privately held corporation is one whose shares are not traded in financial markets. If a private firm has less than 500 shareholders or less than $3 million of assets, registering with the SEC is optional. In general, a private firm is not required to disclose any information to the public or to the SEC. A private corporation can issue stock to a select few. These types of privately held firms are also called closely held firms. Ownership and management is selective, which also means that the shareholders in these firms are not well diversified as they are but a few holding much of one company. Because transparency is lacking with these firms, raising capital is difficult.

5. Reasons a company would pay a stock dividend:

- As a signal of information, such as to reveal good news about the firm's future prospects and not have to spend cash to do so.
- To reduce the price of the stock. Overvalued stocks are subject to higher costs and the payment of a dividend reduces the price of the stock, on average, by the amount of the dividend.

6. The board of directors makes the dividend payment decisions.

Dividend Date Time Line:

- Declaration date: The day the board of directors meets and decides on the dividend.
- Record date: The date specified by the board such that any shareholders who are on record as owning shares on this date are eligible to receive the dividend.
- Ex-dividend date: The date, established by the financial markets as four business days prior to the record date, that determines who receives the dividend (whoever purchased and held on to the shares prior to this date) and who does not (whoever buys the shares on or after this date).
- Payment date: The date the dividend checks are mailed.

7. Reasons for a reverse stock split:

- To raise the price to improve trading and reduce investors' transaction costs for trading in the stock, especially in light of flat commissions which assess the same fees no matter the price of the stock. So theoretically, an investor could pay more for the transaction fees than for the actual stock purchased.
- To raise the price up from a penny stock because penny stocks are viewed negatively.
- As a way to privatize a firm.

8. Reasons a company would repurchase its own stock:

■ To inexpensively distribute cash to shareholders. Shareholders benefit from the tax treatment of capital gains over dividends.
■ To reduce the number of shares outstanding in order to improve earnings per share.
■ To reduce the equity in order to readjust the debt-to-equity ratio. This means that the firm has greater financial leverage, which increases the value of the firm.
■ To creatively and painlessly reduce total dividend payments. The reduction in shares implies a total dividend reduction because the same amount of dividends per share can be paid but for fewer shares.
■ To minimize agency costs by reducing any cash the management can consume as perquisites.
■ To put the firm on a diet. Sometimes firms become too large and unmanageable. When cash is paid out, the value of the firm is reduced.
■ To maximize shareholder wealth. If the firm has no profitable investment opportunities, then it is better to pay funds to the shareholders than to invest in negative NPV projects.

A company would repurchase its own stock using the following methods:

■ A tender offer
■ Open-market purchases
■ A targeted share repurchase

PROBLEMS

Answers

1. a. Dividends per share $= \dfrac{\text{Common stock dividends}}{\text{Number of common shares outstanding}}$

$= \dfrac{\$550,000}{1,300,000} = \$0.42$

b. Dividends payout $= \dfrac{\text{Common stock dividends}}{\text{Available earnings}}$

$\qquad\qquad\qquad = \dfrac{\$550,000}{\$2,400,000} = 0.23 = 23\%$

2. a. Market value = Price per share × Number of shares owned
= $275 × 300 = $82,500

b. After the 3 for 1 stock split, the number of stocks you own has tripled to 900 shares. However the price per share then adjusts accordingly and is approximately $91.67 per share. The market value is still the same: $275/3 × 900 = $82,500.
After the 15% stock dividend, you own 300 × 1.15 = 345 shares. The market value of your investment is still $82,500 as now the shares are worth $275/1.15 = $239.13 per share.

3. Under the ordinary voting procedure, you may cast some or all 500 votes for Ms. W. because one share equals one vote. Under the cumulative voting procedure, you may cast some or all of 500 × 4 = 2000 votes for Ms. W.

CHAPTER 17

Preferred Stock

FILL IN THE BLANKS

Answers

1. preferred; Preferred, income, common; preferred, common; priority, preferred

2. preferred; preferred, first, common; dividends, cash, shares; preferred, quarterly, fixed, floating

3. Fixed, percentage, fixed; variable, adjustable-rate, quarterly, reset; perpetual, collar; issuer, costs, limited, investor, return, lower

4. auction, periodically; Remarketed, agent, tendered, offering; investor, resets, auction, remarketed

5. cumulative, dividend, before, common; noncumulative, not, forgotten, future; cumulative; arrearage, arrears; cumulative

6. conversion, conversion, common, preferred, common; price, ratio, value, common; preferred, premium

7. Callable, buy, shareholder; price; price, set, change, schedule; greater, stated

8. obligation, bondholders, creditors, assurance, sinking; trustee, funds, retire, sinking; preferred, dividend

9. features, package; attractive, cost; issuer, call, investor, conversion; returns, risk, flexibility, costs

SHORT ANSWER QUESTIONS

Answers

1. No longer are only common shareholders allowed to share in the earnings of a firm. Participating preferred stock allows preferred shareholders to share as well. The sharing of earnings is conducted one of two ways, either in addition to the already stated preferred dividend or it can fluctuate along with the dividend for the common stock.

   There are very few participating preferred stock issues because:

   ■ Originally created as a substitute for debt, preferred stock was initially used by firms in failing health. Therefore the cash in hand, by way of dividend, is better than taking a chance on a sick firm's future earnings that may never materialize.

   ■ If a firm has participating preferred stock, it reduces the benefits to common shareholders because regardless of firm health, common shareholders are always the last to receive anything. However in good times, while the common shareholder is still the last to receive, there is at least more to receive after obligations (bondholders and preferred shareholders) are paid.

2. Convertible preferred stock and mandatory preferred stock both give the shareholder the right to exchange the preferred shares for common shares. Convertible preferred stock can convert at a predetermined rate of exchange while mandatory preferred stock must convert within a specified period of time.

   The issuer's perspective on mandatory convertible preferred is that it is beneficial because the firm is freed from its requirement to pay preferred dividends. For the investor, the time limitation on conversion is a cost as the preferred shareholder forfeits the dividend in place of a less profitable and fixed investment.

3. Yes, there are contingent voting rights attached to preferred stock. This means that the right to vote is invoked only when dividends have not been paid for some time. However, this right to vote is very limited.

4. To convert preferred stock into common stock requires investors to consider:

- The uncertainty of the common stock dividend
- The certainty of the preferred dividend
- The unlimited common stock price appreciation
- The limited preferred stock price appreciation

5. Advantages to issuing preferred stock:

- To raise capital in outside markets
- To maintain voting concentration for common shareholders
- Preferred is cheaper and less risky
- Preferred dividends are not taxes

Disadvantages to issuing preferred stock:

- Preferred stockholders have a claim on income and assets.
- Preferred shares have historically been issued by unhealthy firms.

PROBLEMS

Answers

1. Dividend for one year = $1,100,000 \times \$100 \times 8\% = \$8,800,000$

   Arrearage after four years = $\$8,800,000 \times 4 = \$35,200,000$

2. Conversion value = $500 \times 25 \times$ Market price of common share

   Conversion value = $500 \times 25 \times \$30 = \$375,000$

3. Dividends per share = $0.0975(\$80) = \$7.80$ per share, per year

   Total dividends = $\$7.80(\$3,000,000/80) = \$292,500$ per year

CHAPTER 18

Capital Structure

FILL IN THE BLANKS

Answers

1. debt, finance, capital; capital, equity, equity

2. Interest, financial; Financial, decisions, creditors; not

3. debt, equity, creditors; equity, debt, share, return, earnings

4. risk, standard, coefficient; larger, standard, coefficient, greater

5. rate, capitalization, discount, future, value; capitalization, future; uncertain, less, greater

6. premium, discount, income, discount, earnings, interest, free; greater, debt, greater, risk

7. tax shield; marginal, expense; marginal, interest, value

8. exceed, operating; taxes, loss, loss; loss, previous, income

9. limited, assets, debt, risky, creditors, unprofitable; conflict, shareholders', creditors'

10. bankruptcy, direct, indirect; Direct, accounting; indirect, difficult

SHORT ANSWER QUESTIONS

Answers

1. Debt financing is can be more attractive than equity financing because of the interest and principal payments that are required. These steady streams of obligated cash flow (principal and interest payments) indicate the firm is able to maintain these payments as they are guaranteed obligations. All the interest paid is tax deductible. With equity financing, the cash flows (dividends) are neither guaranteed nor tax deductible.

2. Debt ratios differ across industries because the different industries use financial leverage differently. Some industries are prone to financial distress more than others and this is reflected in their ratios. Also, some industries receive tax benefits and are able to capitalize on that which improves their ratios.

   Debt ratios differ within industries since firms within the industry may not be uniform. Also, since subsidiaries financials are subsumed into the parent's financials, the capital structure of the combined may differ from the components. Firms may use differing methods to calculate the ratios, hence the lack of similarity between firms in an industry.

3. The leverage effect is the use of financial leverage. Debt financing requires that principal and interest payments be paid: These payments are not optional. So, if earnings are inadequate, then the firm is obligated to cover these payments through other means and sources of capital. Firms may sell off assets, take on more debt, or issue secondary shares of stock in order to raise the funds to meet the debt payments.

4. The tax shield reduces the net income which is taxable income. Therefore, the value of the firm is being subsidized by the tax shield. The greater the debt, the greater the tax shield deducted from income.

5. The relationship between financial distress and capital structure is of a spiral nature. The more debt a firm takes on, the more of a tax shield they receive. However, the more debt the firm takes on, the less likely it becomes that it will be able to service the debt. When this happens, the firm expends other measures not to default on the debt and hence gets deeper into debt. Eventually the firm goes into financial distress followed by bankruptcy. Factors to be considered are:

■ Causes to increase debt financing
■ Business risk
■ Sales risk
■ Operating risk

6. When making capital structure decisions, financial managers must consider the following factors and ask themselves a multitude of questions:

■ Taxes: Can they benefit? How? Is there enough debt in the mix?
■ Risks: What types? Can they be removed or at least minimized?
■ Type of assets: Do they produce? Can they be liquidated? Is there enough equity in the mix?
■ Financial slack: Is it present? Does the firm need more or less?

PROBLEMS

Answers

1. Firm Z   Debt ratio = $\dfrac{\$34,000}{\$50,000}$ = 0.68

   Debt-to-assets = $\dfrac{\$34,000}{\$84,000}$ = 0.405

Firm Z's debt ratio of 0.68 means that it finances its assets using $0.68 of debt for every $1 of equity. Likewise Firm Z's debt-to-assets ratio means that 40.5% of its assets are financed with debt or alternatively, 40.5 cents of every $1 of assets is financed with debt.

2. Calculation of the capitalization rate for levered Firm Z, with no taxes:

Given:

r_e (unlevered)   = 0.09 or 9%
r_d (risk free debt) = 0.05 or 5%
t_c = 0% (no corporate taxes)

Solve: cost of equity (r_e) for levered firms:

Firm Z:

$$r_e = 0.09 + \left[(0.09 - 0.05)\left(\frac{\$34,000}{\$50,000}\right)\right]$$
$$= 0.09 + [0.04(0.68)]$$
$$= 0.09 + 0.0272$$
$$= 0.117 \text{ or } 11.7\%$$

3. Corporate taxes ($t_c = 25\%$)

	Alternative 1	Alternative 2	Alternative 3
Earnings before interest	$200,000	$200,000	$200,000
Interest	0	50,000	100,000
Earnings after interest	$200,000	$150,000	$100,000
Tax (25%)	50,000	37,500	25,000
Earnings after taxes	$150,000	$112,500	$75,000
Number of shares	÷1,000,000	÷500,000	÷10,000
Earnings per share	$0.15	$0.225	$7.50
Distribution of earnings:			
Earnings to shareholders	$150,000	$112,500	$75,000
Earnings to bondholders	0	50,000	100,000
Earnings to government	+50,000	+37,500	+25,000
Total earnings	$200,000	$200,000	$200,000

4. Calculation of the present value of interest tax shields for different marginal corporate tax rates:

Given:

$D = \$100,000$
$r_d = 0.12 \text{ or } 12\%$

Solve: PVITS (present value of interest tax shield) for various tax rates on corporate income

$$\text{PVITS} = t_c D = 0.12(\$100,000) = \$12,000$$

Management of Cash and Marketable Securities

FILL IN THE BLANKS

Answers

1. operating, generate, assets, risk, current, working; benefits; current, circulating

2. operating; current; manufacture, sell, collect; net, credit; longer, larger

3. out, purchases; into, pay, purchase; cash, cashlike; management, inflows, outflows, cash

4. uncertainty; precautionary, needs, balance; precaution, degree, predict

5. sell, borrow; transaction; transaction, commissions, selling, borrowing, inventory

6. incoming, lockbox, banks, checks, electronic, concentration; clearinghouse; reduce, Federal Reserve; correspondent

7. slowing; controlled, minimizing, immediate, remote, owed, not, increasing, float

8. immediately; certificates, commercial, Eurodollar, Treasury; safety, risks, default, purchasing, interest, reinvestment, liquidity

SHORT ANSWER QUESTIONS

Answers

1. Firms invest in both short-term and long-term assets for the same reason: to maximize owners' wealth. For short-term or current assets, cash flow consideration is a high priority. For long-term assets, both cash flows and the time value of money are priorities. The investment in short-term assets is influenced by many factors. They are:

   ■ Business type
   ■ Product being created
   ■ Operating cycle
   ■ Industry practices
   ■ Customs
   ■ Traditions
   ■ Uncertainty inherent in the business

2. Cash forecasting is exploring the need for cash by investigating short-term estimates, in particular, the method for generating the cash, the quantity needed, and the time frame for getting the cash. In order to fully understand the process, knowledge of the operating cycle and net operating cycle are important. The operating cycle is the time it takes to make cash out of cash. The net operating cycle is the time it takes to make cash from cash plus the time payments are delayed on purchases necessary for production. The net operating cycle is a gauge for the cash to be generated. If the net operating cycle is short, then less cash on hand is needed as cash is generated fairly quickly. The opposite is true for longer net operating cycles.

3. Firms hold cash in order to meet the daily transactions from operations. Each firm must decide how much cash should be held on hand and how it should be administered.

4. The amount or cash balances held depends on the types and sizes of the transactions. Transactions for a grocery store are different from an auto manufacturer. The cash amount also depends on the firm's

operating cycle. During slow times, more cash is needed than during peak periods of production.

Uninvested cash is not earning interest. This is called a holding cost and it is an opportunity cost because the cash could be earning money elsewhere.

5. A lockbox system is a system in which customers can send payments directly to a post office box controlled by the firm's bank, bypassing the firm's processing department. The lockbox system reduces mail float and processing float.

PROBLEMS

Answers

1. a. The average cash balance of the firm, assuming it lets the cash balance drop to zero before cash infusion, is $200,000 ($400,000/2). The holding cost is the lost revenue from investing this cash in short-term securities at 7%. Therefore, the holding cost is:

$$\text{Holding cost} = 0.07(\$200,000) = \$14,000$$

b. The firm needs $1 million each month, so it uses $12 million in a year. The transaction cost is the cost per transaction × the number of transactions in a year. If the firm needs $12 million in a year's time, and each cash infusion is for $400,000, the number of transactions is 30($12,000,000/$400,000). Therefore the transactions costs are:

$$\text{Transactions cost} = \$100 \times 30 = \$3,000$$

c. The cost per transaction is $100, the total demand for cash is $12 million, and the opportunity cost for holding the cash is 7%.

$$Q^* = \sqrt{\frac{2(\$100)(\$12,000,000)}{0.07}} = \$187,164.02$$

Therefore a cash infusion of $185,164 would minimize the costs associated with cash.

2.

  a. The return point is the point at which a new cash infusion should be made. The opportunity cost per day is $0.07/365 = 0.00019$.

  Return point = Lower limit
  $$+ \sqrt[3]{\frac{0.75(\text{Cost per transaction})(\text{Variance of daily cash flows})}{\text{Opportunity cost per day}}}$$
  $$= \left(\$500,000 + \sqrt[3]{\frac{0.75(\$100)(\$75,000)}{0.00019}} \right)$$
  $$= \$503,093.54$$

  Therefore, P&R will need a new cash infusion at $503, 094.

  b. If cash balances exceed the upper limit, the difference between the cash balance and the return point should be invested in marketable securities. Using the Miller-Orr model to calculate the upper limit:

  Upper limit = Lower limit + 3
  $$\times \sqrt[3]{\frac{0.75(\text{Cost per transaction})(\text{Variance of daily cash flows})}{\text{Opportunity cost per day}}}$$
  $$= \left(\$500,000 + 3 \times \sqrt[3]{\frac{0.75(\$100)(\$75,000)}{0.00019}} \right)$$
  $$= \$509,280.63$$

  Therefore P&R will invest in marketable securities when there is cash in excess of $509,281.

3. The lockbox system will free $250,000/day \times 3 days = $750,000 that the firm may invest at 10%. The benefit from this is an additional amount of income of $0.10 \times \$750,000 = \$75,000$. The wire transfers will cost the firm $9,000. This is netted with the processing cost savings, so the additional cost is $9,000 - $5,000 = $4,000. The net benefit to the firm is $75,000 - $4,000 = $71,000. Because this is greater than the cost of the lockbox ($35,000), the system is worthwhile.

4. The order quantity that will minimize total costs for Jewelz is the economic order quantity:

$$Q^* = \sqrt{\frac{2(\text{Cost per transaction})(\text{Total demand})}{\text{Carrying cost per unit}}}$$

$$= \sqrt{\frac{2(\$190)(400{,}000)}{\$7}}$$

$$= 4{,}659.86 = 4{,}660 \text{ stones}$$

Therefore Jewelz is not ordering the optimal amount to minimize its total cost.

CHAPTER 20

Management of Receivables and Inventory

FILL IN THE BLANKS

Answers

1. current, receivable, inventory, operation; inventory, goods, type, nature

2. credit, sales; credit, financial, marketing; sales, services; benefit, profit

3. carrying, holding, opportunity, investment; opportunity, return, opportunity; invested, sales

4. credit, interest; Annualizing, comparable

5. Credit, maximum, payment, discount, discount; discounts, customers, sales, payment, receivable

6. Collection, delinquent; reminders, severe, collection; aggressive, lost

7. Monitoring, receivable, ratios, aging; ratios, receivable; Aging, long, collection

8. credit, benefits, credit, cost; maximizes; uncertain; forecasting, experience

9. Subsidiary, owned, credit, collection; captive, finance, products; sales, loans

10. Inventory; Inventory, sale; factors; investing, insufficient; inventory, little

11. Monitoring, ratios; inventory, inventory; days; sales; demand, production, purchasing; inventory

SHORT ANSWER QUESTIONS

Answers

1. The extension of credit means that customers are allowed to pay for goods and services at a later date after purchase. This type of action creates accounts receivable as the provider of the goods or service is waiting to receive payment. This is also called trade credit which is an informal credit arrangement created in order to increase sales.

2. If a customer pays in full on the purchase date or within the discount period, the customer gets a discount from the invoice price. If the invoice is paid after the discount period, the customer must pay full price. In a sense, this is borrowing because the customer is borrowing the discounted price amount for the price of the discount. For example, if trade credit terms read 5/15, net 30, this means 5% reduction off the invoice if it is paid within 15 days of the purchase, thereafter, the full price is due by the 30th day after purchase. In a sense, if the invoice is $100, then the customer is borrowing $95 for $5. Costs related to granting credit are the cost of the discount, carrying costs (of accounts receivable), administration and collection costs, and risk of default by customers.

3. The following factors must be considered when extending credit:

   ■ The price elasticity of your goods and services
   ■ The probability of bad debts
   ■ Timing of customer's payments

4. The factors that influence the creditworthiness of a firm are capacity, character, collateral, and conditions. Prior experience with customers,

previously assigned credit ratings, consumer reports, and financial condition all underlie these factors. In order for a firm to be deemed creditworthy, they must have high ratings and evidence of the four Cs.

5. Reasons to hold inventory:

   - Need inventory to meet sales
   - Need for staggering stages of produced goods
   - Hold on to speculative inventory
   - To satisfy contractual arrangements

6. The Economic Order Quantity (EOQ) model determines the quantity of inventory to order to minimize total inventory costs (carrying costs + ordering costs). The Economic Order Quantity model makes the following assumptions: (1) Inventory is received instantaneously; (2) inventory is steadily used; and (3) inventory shortages must be avoided.

   The Just-in-Time Inventory (JIT) model is used to cut down on inventory costs by reducing inventory on hand and by coordinating the supply of raw materials with the production and marketing of the goods. The purpose of JIT is to carry no inventory or as little as possible without interfering with production and sales.

PROBLEMS

Answers

1.

   a. If Retton's customers do not take the discount pay on the 60th day, they are, in effect, borrowing the money for $60 - 20 = 40$ days. The discount: $r = 2/98 = 2.041\%$ and there are $365/40 = 9.125$ periods in a year. Therefore, the effective annual rate is:

   $$EAR = (1.02041)^{9.125} - 1 = 20.25\%$$

   If Retton makes the proposed change, the customers will now be paying $3 to borrow $97 for 45 days if they do not take the discount and pay on the 60th day. This makes the discount rate $r = 4/96 = 4.167\%$ and there are $365/45 = 8.11$ periods in a year, so the effective annual rate is $EAR = (1.03093)^{8.11} - 1 = 39.25\%$.

b. The cost to Retton of any discount is equal to the discount percentage times the credit sales using the discount (Retton has not changed its contribution margin).

$$\text{Credit sales using discount} = \text{Sales} \times (\% \text{ using discount})$$
$$= \$500,000 \times 0.6 = \$300,000$$

$$\text{Cost of discount} = \$300,000 \times (0.02) = \$6,000$$

$$\text{Credit sales using discount} = \$800,000 \times (0.75) = \$600,000$$

$$\text{Cost of discount} = \$600,000 \times (0.04) = \$24,000$$

The net cost to Retton of the change in the discount is therefore:

$$\$24,000 - \$6,000 = \$18,000.$$

c. The carrying cost of the receivables is the opportunity cost of Retton's investment in the accounts receivable. Retton's investment is the variable cost of its accounts receivable.

$$\text{Accounts receivable} = \text{ACP} \times \text{Average daily sales}$$
$$= 40 \times \$500,000/365 = \$54,795$$

If the contribution margin is 25%, Retton's variable cost ratio is 75%, so its investment in accounts receivable is $0.75 \times \$54,795 = \$41,096$. So the cost of carrying the receivables is $0.12 \times \$41,096 = \$4,932$.

Under the proposed credit terms, Retton's accounts receivables will be equal to $30 \times 800,000/365 = \$65,753$. Its investment in the accounts receivable is $0.75 \times 65,753 = \$49,315$. So the cost of carrying the receivables is $0.12 \times \$49,315 = \$5,918$. The change in the cost is therefore $\$5,918 - \$4,932 = \$986$.

d. A cost benefit analysis must be done. One benefit is the increased profit due to the increased sales:

$$\text{Benefit from extending credit} = (\text{Contribution margin}) \times (\text{Change in sales})$$
$$= 0.25(\$300,000) = \$75,000$$

A cost is the increase in carrying costs of $986. So the firm enjoys the net benefits of $75,000 - $986 = $74,014. The new credit terms will cost the firm an additional $18,000 in discounts but because the benefits outweigh the costs, Retton should make the change.

CHAPTER 21

Management of Short-Term Financing

FILL IN THE BLANKS

Answers

1. cash, receivable, securities; working, profit; Working, permanent, continual, operations, temporary, difference

2. effective, financing, direct, indirect; funds, compounding

3. Trade, goods, services; Trade, future; seller's, sales; customer's, purchase; seller, receivables, customer, payable

4. payable, purchases; payable, receivable; minimize, credit, sales

5. uniform; customer, better; cost, discount, delayed; beyond, lowers

6. Secured, asset; assets, collateral; collateral, funds; current, marketable, receivable, inventory

7. receivable, secured; receivable, assignment, factoring, securitizing; securitization, short-, intermediate-

8. receivables, receivable, collateral; cash, promissory; amount

9. receivable, collateral, sell, factor; receivables; credit, credit, collecting

10. repurchase, repo; price, date; collateralized, security; repo; overnight, term

SHORT ANSWER QUESTIONS

Answers

1. The costs of borrowing are interest rates and fees. The different types of interest rates and fees are:

   ■ Annual percentage rate is the annualized cost of financing without compounding interest.
   ■ Effective annual rate is the annualized cost of financing with compounding interest.
   ■ A single payment loan is a loan in which everything—principal and interest—is paid at the end of the term.
   ■ A discount loan is a loan for only a portion of the total amount needed by the borrower because the interest is paid in the beginning prior to disbursing the loan.
   ■ Add-on-interest is the traditional idea of a loan in which a portion of the principal and interest is paid each period and interest is compounded.
   ■ Compensating balance is when a specific balance is required at all times.
   ■ A loan origination fee is a fee charged by the lender to perform credit checks and for legal fees in order to process the loan.
   ■ A commitment fee is a fee charged by the lender for the opportunity to use readily available loanable funds.

2. Secured and unsecured financing indicates the existence of collateral in order to guarantee repayment. Often creditworthy customers may be allowed unsecured financing if the lender is satisfied with the customer's ability to pay. If a customer is not creditworthy, then the lender will ask for collateral prior to granting a secured loan.

3. The longer the credit period, the lower the cost of trade credit. This is almost counter-intuitive. However, if one contemplates that the customer/borrower maintains the money that is due to the lender, then the effective annual cost is lowered. The shorter the time the customer/borrower has the money, the higher the effective annual cost

because the customer is, in a sense, not spreading the costs out over a longer period of time.

4. There is no doubt that waiting to pay reduces the cost of trade credit (see the answer to short answer question 3), however if the customer waits too long, then costly penalties can be charged. These penalties range from paying insurance, license fees, late fees, taxes, and bad credit fees.

5. A high turnover is good news if the borrower is reimbursing the sellers in a timely fashion. This establishes goodwill and the sellers will appreciate the prompt payment. High turnover can be bad news if discounts are overlooked as bills are being paid prior to their due date. In this case, the borrower is overpaying the seller twofold—once by paying in a timely manner, and again by paying the discount as a premium. It is as if the borrower is paying for the privilege to pay early.

Low turnover may be good news, as payments are not made too quickly. Granted, discounts cannot be taken advantage of, but the lower effective cost of trade is a benefit. Low turnover can be bad news if payments aren't made in a timely enough fashion and the penalties listed in the answer to short answer question 4 are invoked.

6. The types of financing arrangements:

A single payment loan:

■ is the simplest short-term financing arrangement.
■ utilizes interest rates that are fixed or floating.

A line of credit:

■ is flexible because a bank makes the funds available.
■ has a fixed interest rate.
■ charges a firm a cost regardless of use.
■ has covenants.

A revolving credit agreement:

■ is similar to a line of credit.
■ is for two to three years.
■ allows the borrower to use the credit repeatedly.
■ charges a commitment fee, or compensating balance, and interest.
■ has a floating interest rate.

A letter of credit:

- can be either cancelable or committed by the bank.
- charges the borrower a commitment fee and interest.
- has a fixed interest rate.

There are other loan mechanisms that are sold in the financial markets. They are commercial paper and bankers' acceptances.

Commercial paper:

- comes in large denominations.
- is unsecured.
- is backed by a line of credit from a bank.
- has interest rates that vary.

Bankers' acceptances:

- commit a bank to make payment at maturity if the issuer defaults.
- are used in international trade.
- have maturities of less than 270 days.
- cost a commitment fee and a commission of the interest rate if the issuer defaults.
- have a discount interest rate.

PROBLEMS

Answers

1. The effective annual rate of each alternative must be determined.

   a. The interest charged by Bank A is 16%/4 = 4%, so 0.04 × $100,000 = $4,000. The compensating balance is 0.17 × $100,000 = $17,000. Deducting the compensating balance and the loan origination fee from the face value of the loan leaves CZ with $100,000 – $17,000 – $1,000 = $82,000 of usable funds. The three-month interest rate is then ($4,000 + $1,000)/$82,000 = 6.10%. There are three four-month periods in one year so EAR = $(1.061)^3$ = 19.44%.

b. The interest charged by Bank B is 20%/3 = 6.67%, so 0.0667 × $100,000 = $6,670. The compensating balance is 0.10 × 100,000 = $10,000. Because the loan is a discount loan, the interest is deducted at the beginning of the loan. Deducting the interest and the compensating balance from the face value of the loan leaves CZ with $100,000 − $10,000 − $6,670 = $83,330 of usable funds. The three-month interest rate is $6,670/83,330 = 8.00%. There are four three-month periods in one year so EAR = $(1.08)^4$ = 36.05%.

c. The interest charged by Bank C is 24%/12 = 2%, so 0.02 × 100,000 = $2,000. Because there is no loan origination fee and no compensating balance requirement, CZ has full use of $100,000. The one-month interest rate is $2,000/$100,000 = 2%. There are 12 months in one year so the EAR is $(1.02)^{12} - 1$ = 26.82%.

d. If CZ uses the trade credit, it will forgo $3 in order to borrow $97 for 35 days. The 35-day interest charge is $3/$97 = 3.09%. There are 10.4 35-day periods in one year, the EAR = $(1.0309)^{10.4} - 1$ = 37.23%.

The order of cheapest source to most expensive is: Bank A, Bank C, Bank B, Trade Credit.

2. Safe-T paid $9,700,000 − $9,500,000 = $200,000 to use $9,500,000 for 30 days. The 30-day interest rate is $200,000/$9,500,000 = 2.11%. There are 12.2 30-day periods in one year so the effective annual cost is $(1.0211)^{12.2} - 1$ = 29.01%.

3. The interest on the loan is 0.11 × $1,000,000 = $110,000. The warehouse fee is 0.035 × $1,000,000 = $35,000. Deducting the fee from the proceeds of the loan, Rustee will have $1,000,000 − $35,000 = $965,000 in usable funds. The effective annual cost is ($110,000 + 35,000)/$965,000 = 15.03%.

4. The five-month interest rate is ($250,000 − $237,500)/$237,500 = 5.26%. There are 2.4 five-month periods in a year so the EAR = $(1.0526)^{2.4} - 1$ = 13.09%.

5. We're #1 charges 40 basis points above prime or 4.4% APR. This is a monthly rate of 4.4/12 = 0.37%. There are no other fees so the effective annual rate is $(1.0037)^{12} - 1$ = 4.5%.

We're #2 charges 30 basis points above the prime rate or 4.3% APR. This is a monthly rate of 4.3/12 = 0.36%. The interest fee for the month is then $0.0036 \times 640,000 = \$2,304$. They also charge a fee up front of $0.02 \times \$800,000 = \$16,000$. Chips will save \$4,000 in credit processing costs, however if we assume that these are saved up front, we can net these savings with the fee charged and get $\$16,000 - \$4,000 = \$12,000$. Chips will have usable proceeds from the loan of $\$640,000 - \$12,000 = \$628,000$. The effective monthly cost of the loan is $(\$2,304 + \$12,000)/\$628,000 = 2.28\%$. The EAR = $(1.0228)^{12} - 1 = 31.07\%$.

We're #1's terms are least costly for Bags-O-Chips.

CHAPTER 22

Financial Ratio Analysis

FILL IN THE BLANKS

Answers

1. ratio, ratio, comparison; constructed, characteristic; combinations, statements

2. investment, benefits, investment; assets, power, operating; equity, income, equity

3. return, profit, turnover, Du Pont; components, why, performance

4. Liquidity, short, cash; cash, liquid, current; Current, working, day-to-day

5. operating; operating, cash, services, cash; longer, operating, greater, working

6. profit, income, sales; income, dollar; gross, production; gross, sales

7. Activity, assets, inventory, receivable; inventory, goods, services; receivable, credit; total asset, value, sales

8. risk, debt, debt, equity; leverage, risk; leverage, component, coverage

9. Interest, interest-covered, burdens; interest, debt; greater, better, interest

10. Common-size, statement; common-size, balance, income; calculate, benchmark; balance, assets; income, sales

SHORT ANSWER QUESTIONS

Answers

1. The most basic way of presenting financial information is in ratio format. Ratio analysis can be used to analyze the overall picture of a firm and compare across firms. Ratios are classified according to the characteristic they are measuring:

   ■ A coverage ratio measures "coverage" of financial obligations.
   ■ A return ratio measures net benefit from an investment.
   ■ A turnover ratio measures the functionality of a firm's assets.
   ■ A component percentage is the ratio comparing one amount in a financial statement to the total of the amounts.

2. Five aspects of operating performance that should be analyzed for overall viability of the firm are:

   ■ Return on investment
   ■ Liquidity
   ■ Profitability
   ■ Activity
   ■ Financial leverage

   It is important to know whether or not the firm is functioning to its best capacity and if assets are being used properly in order to obtain the goal of maximizing shareholder wealth.

3. The Du Pont system measures the source of performance. It does so by decomposing return ratios into components that identify which area is responsible for the performance.

4. Book value is an accounting measure and involves past values. It does not capture the dynamic value as seen by the market and what an investor is likely to pay. Because the two measures are different by nature, book value and market value are not highly correlated.

5. Financial ratio analysis tells a partial story based on book values. It does not necessarily tell the entire story. There are many limitations of ratio analysis and this needs to be considered when attempting to analyze a firm. Other concerns arise with the methods and data used in forecasting and in the selection of the correct benchmark. Keep in mind that accounting data can be unreliable and can only tell so much.

PROBLEMS

Answers

1. Recall, data from financials are assumed to be × $100,000. Overall, we can see that Wang is struggling to recover after bankruptcy.

a. Current ratio = $\dfrac{\$425,000}{\$381,000}$ = 1.12 times

b. Quick ratio = $\dfrac{\$401,000}{\$381,000}$ = 1.05 times

c. Inventory turnover = $\dfrac{\$656,000}{\$24,000}$ = 27.33 times

d. Total asset turnover = $\dfrac{\$946,000}{\$859,000}$ = 1.10 times

e. Gross profit margin = $\dfrac{\$946,000 - 656,000}{\$946,000}$ = 30.7%

f. Operating profit margin = $\dfrac{-\$63,000}{\$946,000}$ = −6.66%

g. Net profit margin = $\dfrac{-\$58,000}{\$946,000}$ = −6.13%

h. Debt-to-assets ratio $= \dfrac{\$494,000}{\$859,000} = 57.61\%$

i. Debt-to-equity ratio $= \dfrac{\$494,000}{\$366,000} = 135\%$

j. Return on assets (basic earning power) $= \dfrac{-\$63,000}{\$859,000} = -7.33\%$

k. Return on equity $= \dfrac{-\$58,000}{\$366,000} = -15.8\%$

l. Average day's cost of goods sold $= \dfrac{\$656,000}{365 \text{ days}} = \$1,797 \text{ per day}$

Number of days of inventory $= \dfrac{\$24,000}{\$1,797 \text{ per day}} = 13.36 \text{ days}$

m. Assuming all sales on credit:

Credit sales per day $= \dfrac{\$946,000}{365 \text{ days}} = \$2,592 \text{ per day}$

Number of days credit $= \dfrac{\$182,000}{\$2,592} = 70.22 \text{ days}$

n. Assuming all purchases on credit:

Average days purchases $= \dfrac{\$656,000 - 134,000}{365 \text{ days}} = \$1,430 \text{ per day}$

Number of days of purchases $= \dfrac{\$381,000}{\$1,430} = 266.43 \text{ days}$

o. Operating cycle = 13.36 days + 70.22 days = 83.58 days

p. Net operating cycle = 83.58 – 266.43 days = –182.85 days

2. The industry ratios:

Current ratio	2 times
Quick ratio	1 times
Number of days of credit	90 days
Inventory turnover	35 times
Total asset turnover	3 times
Debt-to-equity ratio	45%
Operating profit margin	10%
Net profit margin	7%
Return on assets	9%
Return on equity	11%

Wang's ratios:

Current ratio	1.12 times
Quick ratio	1.05 times
Number of days of credit	30 days
Inventory turnover	27.33 times
Total asset turnover	1.10 times
Debt-to-equity ratio	135.0%
Operating profit margin	–6.66%
Net profit margin	–6.13%
Return on assets	–7.33%
Return on equity	–15.8%

All in all, Wang is still struggling to emerge from bankruptcy. The current ratio and the quick ratios do show that Wang can cover current obligations. However, that is about all they can do until they can regain their financial footing. They do have fewer number of days of credit, which implies that they want to receive customer payments sooner, and while extending credit does increase sales, Wang might be able to lengthen the number of days after it gets in better shape. Currently, the cash flow from accounts receivable is in demand by the company. Wang is carrying entirely too much debt and turnover is too slow relative to the industry. They have negative profit margins and returns indicating they are losing money. Management needs to take a hard look at what it can do to improve the firms financial health or else it may want to consider filing for Chapter 22 (Chapter 11 for the second time).

CHAPTER 23

Earnings Analysis

FILL IN THE BLANKS

Answers

1. prices; future, forecasted, stock; stock, over, under

2. Forecasting; historical, current, earnings, dividends; value

3. operations, operating, EBIT; overall, net income, less; common shareholder's, preferred

4. amount, dollar; income, share, market; EPS, common, outstanding

5. Basic; Diluted, dilutive; earnings, restate

6. future, cash, prices; publicly, analysts; providers, forecasts

7. consensus, average; surprise, actual, forecasted, forecasted

8. Consensus, individual, explaining, momentum, torpedo; growth, current, next

9. future, previous, autoregressive; time, historical, adjusted; statistical, previously

10. earnings; price-earnings, P/E; price, earnings; stock, earnings; inverse, yield, E/P

SHORT ANSWER QUESTIONS

Answers

1. The market price of a share of stock is dictated by the price paid for it. The price is the reflection of investors' beliefs concerning the future stream of cash flows.

2. Earnings management is when financial information is manipulated (through accounting methods, inventory methods, depreciation methods, and timing) so the financials look better than they actually are. In other words, earnings management attempts to paint a rosier picture of a firm that may have something to hide or else just wants to outshine its competitors. The financial analyst must be very familiar with the business practices and their methods in order to provide accurate information to investors.

3. The relationship between earnings and stock price is as follows:

   ■ Stock prices rise or fall in response to an announcement of unexpected good or poor earnings.
   ■ Accounting earnings are correlated more with long-term stock returns than short-term stock returns.

   The source of this relationship is unclear. Some believe that the strong relationship is because earnings are not managed and others believe reported earnings drive stock price.

4. Earnings per share is influenced by the changing number of common shares outstanding. Changes in shares outstanding occur because of:

   ■ Timing: Since the number of shares outstanding changes constantly, this movement is highly dynamic compared to the net income that is earned over the same time. So for any given company, it may show a variety of EPS measures throughout the year because the number of shares is constantly in flux, however the EPS measures are calculated at specified intervals.
   ■ Dilutive securities: The existence of convertible securities such as convertible preferred stock, employee stock options, convertible bonds, and warrants are exercised at different times thus changing the number of shares that influence the denominator of the EPS ratio.

The changing number of common shares outstanding is the cause for the multiple forms of EPS:

■ Basic earnings per share (BPS) are earnings minus preferred dividends, divided by the average number of shares outstanding.
■ Diluted earnings per share (DPS) are earnings minus preferred dividends, divided by the number of shares outstanding considering all dilutive securities.

5. The accuracy of EPS forecasts depends completely upon the validity of the data, the quantity of data (meaning the number of years' worth of data) and the type of statistical method. Often the data used in forecasting EPS are historical EPS of the company, however, the EPS measures must be recalculated based on the adjustments in accounting policy. Forecasting based on trends of EPS can be precarious and is model dependent, and the results should be interpreted with extreme caution. There is conflicting literature concerning the value of financial analysts' forecasts. Some hold that analyst forecasts are not any better than the currently used statistical models and others say they are better because analysts can process the current information and apply human reasoning. The point is that the accuracy of the forecast is only as good as the data, the model, and the modeler, which leaves much room for doubt and mistakes. Don't kill the analysts, they are only human.

PROBLEMS

Answers

1. Finding the earnings per share (EPS) for the end of the year:

$$\text{Earnings per share} = \frac{\text{Earnings available to common stockholders}}{\text{Number of common shares outstanding}}$$

$$\text{EPS} = \frac{\$6.5 \text{ million}}{1.87 \text{ million}} = \$3.48 \text{ per share}$$

This is a rough measure as it does not consider time. If time is considered, then the estimate for EPS changes.

Q1 = 1.5 million shares outstanding, Q2 = Q3 = Q4 = 1.87 million shares, then

$$\text{EPS} = \frac{\$6.5 \text{ million}}{0.25(1.5 \text{ million shares}) + 0.75(1.87 \text{ million})}$$

$$= \frac{\$6.5 \text{ million}}{1,777,500 \text{ shares outstanding}}$$

$$= \$3.67 \text{ per share}$$

2. a. Dividend Payout Ratio

$$= \frac{\text{Dividends}}{\text{Earnings available to common shareholders}}$$

$$= \frac{\$0.30}{\$1.80} = 16.7\%$$

b. P/E ratio $= \dfrac{\text{Market price per share}}{\text{Earnings per share}} = \dfrac{\$28.50}{\$1.80} = 15.83$

c. Investors base their purchase decisions on expected future earnings, not on past earnings. The P/E ratio indicates how much investors are willing to pay for each dollar of current earnings per share. It does not take future earnings into account, but investors do. It can be shown that sometimes investors are too optimistic and have paid for overvalued stock.

3.

$$\text{BPS} = \frac{\text{Earnings available to common shareholders} - \text{Preferred dividends}}{\text{Number of shares outstanding}}$$

$$\text{DPS} = \frac{\text{Earnings available to common shareholders} - \text{Preferred dividends}}{\text{Number of shares outstanding including all dilutive securities}}$$

Because there is no specific method of timing, weighted measures are not used.

$$\text{BPS} = \frac{\$4,355 \text{ million}}{1,300 \text{ million shares outstanding}} = \$3.35 \text{ per share}$$

DPS

$$= \frac{\$4{,}355 \text{ million}}{1{,}300 \text{ million shares outstanding} + 300 \text{ million potentially dilutive shares}}$$

= $2.72 per share

4. a. Forecast error $= \dfrac{\text{Actual EPS} - \text{Consensus EPS}}{\text{Actual EPS}}$

$$= \frac{\$1.82 - \$1.95}{\$1.82} = -7.14\%$$

b. The forecast error is –7.14%, meaning that the actual was 7.14% lower than the forecasted. The market will react negatively to the worse-than-expected earnings and the stock price should decrease accordingly.

CHAPTER 24

Cash Flow Analysis

FILL IN THE BLANKS

Answers

1. Cash, valuation, value, future; past, current, dividends, expenditure, financing

2. measuring, into, out; cash, size, demands, working

3. nondiscretionary, discretionary; statement, flexibility, decisions, health

4. no, calculating; measure, methods, calculate

5. net free, NFCF; earnings, less; expenditures, maintenance, expansion, working

6. Net, unconstrained; creditor's, ability, debt; shareholder's, reinvested

7. capital expenditures, capital expenditures; flexibility, capital; larger, greater

8. debt, debt, debt; ability, debt, credit

9. information, condition; Healthy, unhealthy, operations, declining; unhealthy, more

SHORT ANSWER QUESTIONS

Answers

1. There is no uniform definition of cash flow, so it must always be discussed in context. Cash flow can be the total amount of cash flowing into and out of the company during a period. It can be the net of those cash flows. Some ways to measure cash flow are:

   ■ Add noncash expenses to net income
   ■ Calculate earnings before interest, taxes, depreciation, and amortization
   ■ Use the statement of cash flows

2. The direct method of reporting cash flow is reporting all cash inflows and outflows. The indirect method begins with net income and makes adjustments for depreciation, noncash expenses, and changes in working capital. Of the two, the direct method is the most computationally expensive.

3. Examining the cash flows from operations, investments, and financing activities, an analyst can gauge the activities of the firm. Please refer to Exhibit 24.1 on page 802 of *Financial Management and Analysis* for more detail.

4. Michael Jensen developed the theory of free cash flow which is the cash flow left over after the company funds all positive NPV projects. In other words, free cash flow is the cash flow of the firm, less capital expenditures necessary to stay in business and grow at the expected rate. Free cash flow reveals how firms actually get rid of their excess cash. This can be done through dividend payments to shareholders, retirement of debt, repurchase of stock, and the like. If free cash flow is not purged, the firm holding the free cash flow could become a takeover target by a firm that needs free cash flow.

5. An analysis of cash flows can reveal a more accurate picture of a firm's health and operations. The analysis reveals:

   ■ The sources of financing for the company's capital spending
   ■ The company's dependence on borrowing
   ■ The quality of earnings

PROBLEMS

Answers

1. Although there are several variations on how to calculate the various free cash flows, the method that is applied to this problem can be found on page 808 of *Financial Management and Analysis*. The purpose of choosing this method is to keep the calculations simple.

Free Cash Flows	In Millions
EBIT	$21
Depreciation and amortization	$4
Capital expenditures	($15)
Free cash flow	$10
Interest	($2)
Taxes	($7)
Net free cash flow	$1
Cash dividends	($2)
Net cash flow	($1)

CHAPTER 25

International Financial Management

FILL IN THE BLANKS

Answers

1. domestic; financing, investment, international, domestic; financial, global

2. protectionism; Agreement, Tariffs, barriers; International Monetary, IMF; European, economic; American, Trade, NAFTA, goods

3. multinational, countries; multinational, borders; domestic, markets, production, resources, hurdles, technology

4. currencies; exchange, currency; exchange, currency, value; exchange-rate, adversely

5. loses, depreciated, devalued; gains, appreciated, revalued

6. no, price, same; one, currencies, price; purchasing power, PPP

7. Income, indirect, central, corporate; sales, business

8. subsidiaries; intercompany, transfer; congruence, multinational; taxes, income, import

9. Globalization, integration; internal, national, external; domestic, foreign; domestic, domiciled, traded

10. segmented, integrated; segmented, not; integrated, no; neither, mildly, mildly

11. bond, foreign, Euromarket; underwritten, simultaneously, outside, unregistered; Eurobond

12. cost, international, domestic, international; foreign, repatriation, political; restrictions, capital

SHORT ANSWER QUESTIONS

Answers

1. As the global community gets smaller and more easily accessible, firms should participate in the international market for the sake of survival, competition, and increasing profits. Because everything today is more global, a firm in isolation will have trouble competing. If firms cannot compete, they do not survive. The goal of the firm is to maximize shareholder wealth and with the advent of computers and advanced telecommunications, this can be done through worldwide expansion in friendly markets.

2. Free trade is the ability of countries to trade with one another without being constrained. Free trade promotes specialization which makes production more efficient and increases output. This in turn increases competition which translates into product variety and lower prices for the consumer. Free trade benefits countries that have a comparative or competitive advantage, however it hurts those that don't.

3. Corporate income tax is based on a percentage of income earned. The rate can vary within the country, such as in the United States where there are tax brackets, and it can vary between countries. If a company has foreign branches and/or subsidiaries, it is customary for resident corporations to be taxed by the main country on the entire worldwide income. Some countries repatriate taxes, meaning they return some of the taxes back to the country in which the subsidiary resides. If a company is a nonresident corporation, then that company

only pays taxes on the income earned within the country. Some countries have tax treaties that allow for negotiation of tax treatments.

4. There is no set global definition of taxable income, therefore it varies from country to country. Nonresident corporations and expatriates often must obtain an accountant in the foreign country and one in their home country in order to fully determine taxable income because there are multiple methods in dealing with some of the accounting data. Such items that are treated differently are depreciation, inventory, the deductibility of interest expense, and inflation of expenses.

5. When a corporation issues equity outside of its domestic market and it is traded in the foreign market, it is an international depository receipt (IDR). Banks issue IDRs as proof of ownership and hold them in trust for the owner. A benefit to the IDR is that the issuer is released from foreign regulatory issuing requirements.

   The American depository receipt (ADR), is the U.S. version of the IDR. Characteristics of ADRs are:

   ■ They are denominated in U.S. dollars.
   ■ They pay dividends.
   ■ They do not grant the holder voting rights or any rights that give authority in the company.

PROBLEMS

Answers

1. A Venezuelan bolivar is worth $0.000626 U.S.
   An Australian dollar is worth $0.64 U.S.

   a. There are 0.64/$0.0006 = 1,066.67 Venezuelan bolivars per Australian dollar

   b. There are $0.0006/$0.64 = 0.0009375 Australian dollars per Venezuelan bolivars

2. Consider, $10,000 (35,000 ARS):

$$\text{In terms of AR: Return} = \frac{43,750 - 35,000}{35,000} = 25\%$$

$$\text{In terms of US\$: Return } = \frac{\$12,500 - 10,000}{\$10,000} = 25\%$$

a. Return $= \dfrac{\$875 - 10,000}{\$10,000} = -91.25\%$

b. Return $= \dfrac{\$21,875 - 10,000}{\$10,000} = 1.19\%$

3. a. Transfer price = $30

	U.S. Parent Company Alone	Subsidiary
Revenue	$6,000,000	$38,000,000
Variable manufacturing costs	$4,000,000	$9,000,000
Fixed manufacturing costs	$3,000,000	$2,000,000
Taxable income	($1,000,000)	$27,000,000
Income taxes	0	$12,150,000
Net income after taxes	($1,000,000)	$14,850,000

Worldwide income taxes: $12,150,000

Worldwide net income after taxes: $13,150,000

b. Transfer price $50

	U.S. Parent Company Alone	Subsidiary
Revenue	$10,000,000	$38,000,000
Variable manufacturing costs	$4,000,000	$13,000,000
Fixed manufacturing costs	$3,000,000	$2,000,000
Taxable income	$3,000,000	$23,000,000
Income taxes	$900,000	$10,350,000
Net income after taxes	$2,100,000	$12,650,000

Worldwide income taxes: $10,350,000

Worldwide net income after taxes: $14,750,000

Borrowing via Structured Finance Transactions

FILL IN THE BLANKS

Answers

1. bond, loans, receivables; collateral, asset; finance, structured

2. structured, asset; bond, asset, funding; all-in-cost, lower

3. credit, asset; rating, ability, equity; loan; determinant, default, sell, loan

4. third, servicer, originator; payments, delinquencies, finance

5. Rating, servicer, servicer, credit; servicer, not, backup

6. structure, flows, payments, obligations; losses, rate; stress, risk, not, credit, credit

7. enhancement, fee, insurance, yield, credit; External, credit; Internal, senior; more, specific

8. easiest, insurance; insurance, guarantee; event; downgraded, downgraded

9. senior, internal, bond; several; yield, yields; lower, more, lower

10. Reserve, cash, spread; Cash; deposited, offset; spread, coupon, fee, expenses

SHORT ANSWER QUESTIONS

Answers

1. Structured finance refers to debt and related securities that are backed by collateral such as loans or receivables or third-party support. To make use of a structured financing, a lender would accumulate loans or receivables and use them as collateral for debt securities the lender would then issue. Therefore, the debt obligation that the lender issues is backed by the proposed incoming cash flows from the loans being paid into the lender or any accounts receivables.

2. The purposes for using structured financing are as follows:

   - Potential for reducing funding costs
   - To diversify funding sources
   - To accelerate earnings for financial reporting purposes
   - For regulated entities, potential relief from capital requirements
   - The tax treatment of sales to special purpose vehicles

3. A captive finance company is usually a subsidiary whose sole purpose is to provide financing to customers who buy the parent company's products. Often the types of companies that utilize captive finance companies are manufacturers, however some retailers also will do this with what sounds like in-store-credit, however the outside credit provider is a captive finance company.

4. Credit rating agencies investigate:

   - The collateral's credit quality
   - The quality of the seller/servicer
   - Cash flow stress and payment structure

   Verification of overall credit quality only comes after the rating agencies scrutinize the borrower's ability to service the obligations and the borrower's equity in the asset. Everything about the borrower comes under review from the servicing history to the financial condition of the borrower. If the borrower receives an acceptable rating, the borrower is free to obtain a structured financing; if not, then either the borrower must seek third-party credit help or give up on the structured financing.

CHAPTER 27

Equipment Leasing

FILL IN THE BLANKS

Answers

1. lease, lease, payments; lessor, lessee

2. Equipment, nontax, tax; Nontax, conditional sale, price, renewal; tax, lessor, lessee

3. advantage, leasing, lessees, conserves; borrows, equal; borrowing, equity, payment

4. payment, equipment, creditworthiness, economic; Leasing; delivery, installation; lease

5. standards, capital, liability, balance; operating, not; footnote, financial; capital, operating

6. cancelable, obsolescence; avoidance, cost; disposal, lessor; value, cost

7. covenants, restrictions, loan; true, Internal Revenue, true, loan

8. true, lower, superior; after-tax, superior; true, less, book, depreciation, interest

9. commercial, subsidiaries, leasing, captive, finance, investment, insurance

10. indirectly, working; Captive, subsidiaries, parent; Captives, lease

11. brokers, advisers, equipment; pricing, structuring, negotiating; lessees, lessor; brokerage; complexity, attractiveness, environment

12. synthetic, ownership, investor; off-balance, cost

SHORT ANSWER QUESTIONS

Answers

1. A typical leasing transaction works as follows: The lessee first decides all the particulars on the necessary equipment and the terms of delivery. Negotiations are made on the price and sales contract, including the lease agreement and the specifics. After signing of the lease, the equipment is delivered and paid for. When the term of the lease has concluded, the lessee may renew, buy the equipment outright, or return the equipment.

2. The leveraged form of a true lease of equipment is the ultimate form of lease financing. Its selling point (or leasing point) is the ability of the lessor to benefit from the tax treatment of depreciation while the lessee receives the lease at a lower cost.

3. Leasing is an alternative to purchasing, with benefits. Because it is similar to a debt obligation, the debt payments can be used by the lessee to conserve capital. Leasing is less expensive than purchasing, it preserves credit and avoids the risk of being saddled with obsolete equipment that will need to be disposed of. In general, leases are flexible for a variety of reasons, some of which are:

   ■ They are less restrictive.
   ■ They can be customized.
   ■ Financing is easily obtained.
   ■ Disclosure is unnecessary.
   ■ There is no maintenance.
   ■ There is less impact on cash flow.

4. There are two types of leases: operating leases and capital leases. Characteristics of operating leases are that there is no complete

transfer of ownership—the leased property is not capitalized, the lease is not reported on the balance sheet, lease payments are expensed, and they must be disclosed in the financial statements. A capital lease is leasing an asset but treating it as if it is purchased and financed over a designated period. Unlike operating leases, capital leases must be reported as a liability on the balance sheet. Further, there is a transfer of ownership and the lessee is allowed to receive the tax benefits of depreciation.

PROBLEMS

Answers

1. a. Depreciation amounts:

Year	Depreciation
1	$49,995
2	66,675
3	22,215
4	11,115

b. Cost of the machine: $150,000
Tax credit: 0
Estimated pretax residual: $5,000 value after disposal costs
Economic life of the machine: 5 years

	End of Year				
	0	1	2	3	4
Cost of machine	150,000				
Lost tax credit	0	0	0	0	0
Lease payment	(35,000)	(35,000)	(35,000)	(35,000)	
Tax shield form lease payment[a]	10,500	10,500	10,500	10,500	
Lost depreciation tax shields[b]		(14,999)	(20,003)	(6,665)	(3,335)
Lost residual value					(3,500)
Total	125,500	(39,499)	(44,503)	(31,165)	(6,835)

[a] Lease payment multiplied by the marginal tax rate.
[b] Depreciation for year multiplied by marginal tax rate.

c. Adjusted discount rate = $(1 - 0.30) \times (0.12) = 0.084 = 8.4\%$.

d. Value of the lease:

End of Year	Net Cash Flow from Lease	Present Value
0	$125,500	-$125,500
1	-39,499	-36,438
2	-44,503	-37,873
3	-31,165	-24,467
4	-6,835	-4,950
Net present value of leasing cash flows		$21,272

e. Loan amortization:

Year	Loan Balance at Beginning of Year	Loan Payment	Interest (Beginning Loan Balance × 12%)	Reduction in Loan Principal	Loan Balance End of Year
0	$150,000	$49,385	$18,000	$31,385	$118,615
1	118,615	49,385	14,234	35,131	83,484
2	83,484	49,385	10,018	39,367	44,117
3	44,117	49,385	5,294	44,091[a]	100[a]

[a] Differences due to rounding, if three decimal places are maintained, the loan balance goes to zero.

CHAPTER 28

Project Financing

FILL IN THE BLANKS

Answers

1. Structured, value; securitization, balance; vehicle, SPV, asset, securities

2. corporations, flow, corporations; project, SPV

3. lender, flows, repayment, paid, worst; guarantees

4. moving, sponsor; sponsors; construction, construction, operation, operating, profit; processing, distribution

5. loans, sponsor, credit, balance; third; independently

6. lenders, operation, time, produce, amounts, plan; startup

7. return, invested, leveraging, commercial; parties, debt, direct, indirect

8. Tax, depreciation, interest, depletion, research, dividends, foreign, capital, debt; benefits

9. new, taxes, transferred, use; 80%, consolidation, foreign, 50%

SHORT ANSWER QUESTIONS

Answers

1. Project financing is attractive when the balance sheet remains unaffected and does not influence the credit rating of the sponsoring party. Project financing allows for highly leveraged projects to take place when they wouldn't otherwise.

2. There are varying credit exposures that arise throughout a project financing in the engineering and construction phase, startup phase, and operations phase.

   A variety of guarantees and business partners can be utilized though the life of the project financing in order to maintain the appropriate credit support.

3. Risks must be identified, evaluated, examined, and evaded during the project in order to avoid project failures. Some common causes for project failures include the following:

   - Delay in completion
   - Cost overrun
   - Technical failure
   - Financial failure
   - Uninsured losses
   - Increased price or material shortages
   - Technical obsolescence
   - Loss of competitive edge
   - Poor management
   - Actual value of security is too low

4. Nonrecourse borrowing by third parties is structured in ways so that the third party's (or sponsor's) credit standing and balance sheet are relatively unaffected. This is often done by using a third party's credit rating or using multiple parties' credit ratings. When multiple backers for a project all have good credit ratings, this secures the lender's confidence that the project is viable and the risk for default is minimized. For the backers, the project risk is likewise minimized by sharing.

5. Benefits and incentives for project financings are:

- Availability of credit sources
- Availability of guarantees
- Better credit terms and interest costs
- Achieve higher leverage
- Meet legal requirements
- Regulatory problems avoided
- Segregated costs
- Financial statements unaffected until completion

Disincentives for project financing are:

- Complexity
- Complicated documentation
- Higher cost of borrowing funds
- Challenging negotiations with multiple parties

CHAPTER 29

Strategy and Financial Planning

FILL IN THE BLANKS

Answers

1. economic, forecasting, accounting; Economic, marketing, production, sales, costs; Accounting, summarize, project

2. comparative, producing, distributing; competitive; invest, more, return

3. strategy, maximizing; positive net present; objectives; strategic; financial, opportunities

4. Sales; Inaccurate, inventory, financing; misses, understating, overstating, problems

5. cash, economic, industry, market; uncertainty; sales, regression, market, opinions

6. familiarity, products, customers, competitors, future; expertise, evaluate; problems; persuade, allocate

7. Forecasting, short, long; people; optimistic, rosier, future; past, weight; responsible, rewarding, penalizing

8. budgeting, cash, income, balance; cash, most, income, balance; credit, coincide

9. pro forma, projected, future; income, income, revenues, expenses; investment, financing

10. analysis, cash; pro forma, asset, liability, equity; percent-of-sales, sales, income, sales, balance

SHORT ANSWER QUESTIONS

Answers

1. Financial planning is the allotment of resources to meet investment goals. Financial planning is important as it gives insight into the manager's decisions as to their perception of market conditions and how the dynamic market conditions will affect the investing and financing decisions of the company.

2. The firm's investment plans and financing plans mentioned in short answer question 1 are the firm's budgeting process. Operational budgeting refers to short-term budgeting and long-run planning is long-term budgeting.

   Budgeting determines feasible investments based on the current ability to finance them. Budgets gauge current and past performance of departments, divisions, or individual managers.

3. Regression is a mathematical model fitting technique that fits a line graphically expressing the relationship between two units. Regression is used to forecast based on historical data. Forecasting errors are the difference between the forecasted value and the actual value.

4. Analysis of cash flows allows the tracking of cash inflows and outflows as a result of operating, investing, and financing activities. Cash inflows should be greater than cash outflows. A cash budget, which is a detailed statement of the cash flows expected in future periods, can help identify financing and investment needs.

5. There are many analyses and forecasting techniques for cash flows. Each one is subject to its own prescribed assumptions concerning a variety of factors such as the economic conditions, market conditions, and other factors affecting cash flows. Two methods mentioned in the text that help gauge uncertainty of cash flows are sensitivity analysis

and simulation analysis. Sensitivity analysis is the changing of one variable at a time and examining its effect on all the other components. When more than one variable is changed at a time, this involves simulation analysis.

PROBLEMS

Answers

1. DoReMi Company:

Without adjustment:

$$\text{Current ratio} = \frac{\$500 + 300 + 300}{\$525} = 2.10$$

$$\text{Debt-to-equity ratio} = \frac{\$525 + 575}{\$525} = 2.75$$

With adjustments:

The cash account and, in turn, accounts payable, are the easiest and quickest to adjust. The other accounts can be altered accordingly and this should be taken into consideration for the long-term plan of the company. However in the interim, for the pro forma balance sheet for next month, the cash account can be easily reduced to adjust the current ratio, by the following amount:

$$\text{With adjustment, current ratio} = \frac{\$500 - x + 300 + 300}{\$525 - x}$$
$$= \frac{\$1,100 - x}{\$525 - x} = 4.0$$

Using algebra to solve for X, $\$X = 333$. If DoReMi reduces cash by $333 (paying off $333 of short-term liabilities), the current ratio requirement is satisfied.

With adjustment to the cash account, the debt-to-equity ratio falls in line below 2 to 1.92.

Assets		Liabilities and Equities	
Cash	$167	Accounts payable	$192
Accounts receivable	300	Long-term debt	575
Inventory	300	Common equity	400
Plant and equipment	400	Total liabilities and equity	$1,167
Total assets	$1,167		

The cash balance may be less than what is needed for transaction purposes, thus introducing the risk of not having sufficient cash on hand.

Other means of reducing the current ratio are to (1) reduce accounts receivable (by not extending as much credit or being more aggressive in collections), which risks hurting future sales; or (2) reduce levels of inventory, which risks not having sufficient inventory to meet demand.

In addition, the firm can borrow using long-term debt (increasing its financial leverage) to add to its current accounts, increasing its current ratio. But this increases the financial risk of the firm and may increase the cost of debt and equity.

2.

Month	Sales	Collection of Month's Sales	Collection on Previous Month's Sales	Collection on Sales from Two Months Previous	Total Collections from July–Sept. Sales
July	$12,000	$2,400	from June	from May	$2,400
August	$20,000	$4,000	$6,720	from June	$8,720
September	$15,000	$3,000	$11,200	$2,800	$17,000

3. The predicted current, plant, and total assets are as follows:

	Base Year	As a % of Base Year Sales	Projected
Current assets	$200,000	20%	$280,000
Plant assets	500,000	50%	700,000
Total assets	$700,000	70%	$980,000